Java
Programming Projects
ACTIVITIES WORKBOOK

CEP, Inc.

John Sestak

VISIT US ON THE INTERNET
www.swep.com

South-Western Educational Publishing

an International Thomson Publishing company I(T)P®

www.thomson.com

Cincinnati • Albany, NY • Belmont, CA • Bonn • Boston • Detroit • Johannesburg • London • Madrid
Melbourne • Mexico City • New York • Paris • Singapore • Tokyo • Toronto • Washington

Library of Congress Cataloging-in-Publication Data
Sestak, John.
    Java programming projects / John Sestak.
      p.   cm.
    ISBN 0-538-69404-1
    1. Java (Computer program language).   I. Title.

  QA76.73.J38 S43   2001
  005.2'762—dc21   99-048316
                                                                      CIP

Managing Editor:	Carol Volz
Production Manager:	Dave Lafferty
Consulting Editor	Custom Editorial Productions, Inc.
Marketing Manager:	Larry Qualls
Design Coordinator:	Mike Broussard
Production:	Custom Editorial Productions, Inc.

You can request permission to use material from this text through the following phone and fax numbers: Phone: 1-800-730-2214, Fax: 1-800-730-2215, or visit our web site at http://www.thomsonrights.com

ISBN: 0-538-69404-1

5 6 7 8 9 10 MZ 08 07 06 05 04 03 02

Printed in the United States of America

International Thomson Publishing

South-Western Educational Publishing is a division of International Thomson Publishing, Inc. The ITP registered trademark is used under license.

The purpose of this project book is to reinforce the topics that you have been exposed to in your Java class. It is intended to support the textbook from which you have been learning theory. The projects in this book are "Java-oriented," meaning each program should run on any compiler. Any specific code sequences that are meant to be run on one compiler will be noted.

Programming expertise comes from using the materials that have been presented to you over and over again. The old adage that "practice makes perfect" definitely holds true when dealing with programming. And that is the purpose of this book—to give you the opportunity to practice, practice, practice!

Using This Book

The programs you develop in this book will work whether you are using Microsoft's Visual J++ 6.0, Borland's Jbuilder, Sun Java, or a simple text editor.

Each project and end-of-lesson application and Critical Thinking exercise is identified as either a beginner (B), intermediate (I), or advanced (A) level activity. You will also notice that some exercises are marked with a SCANS icon. *SCANS* stands for the "Secretary's Commission on Achieving Necessary Skills." A SCANS icon next to an exercise indicates that it satisfies a majority of the workplace competency and foundation skills identified by the commission.

This book is accompanied by the Electronic Instructor CD. This invaluable resource contains printouts of the code for each program you create, answers to project and end-of-lesson Review Questions, and other components designed to enhance the learning experience.

Acknowledgments

I would like to thank God for providing me with the ability to share my knowledge with others. I would like to thank Roseann Krane for her insightful review of the manuscript, and Tom Bockerstette for his thorough technical review. I'd like to thank Betsy Newberry, and the rest of the staff at Custom Editorial Productions, Inc., and South-Western Educational Publishing for their belief in my ability to actually create this book. I would like to thank Paul J. Deitel of Deitel & Associates for making me a true believer in Java and for providing me with the knowledge to start on the path to becoming a true Java programmer!

Last, but certainly not least, I would like to thank my wife, Trish, and our three rugrats, Ryan, Kristi, and Tim, for working with me—and around me—as this book developed. I would also like to add my thanks to my mom and dad, who keep involved with everything I do. You realize that accomplishments become more meaningful when you have family that you can share them with.

John Sestak
Microsoft Certified Professional
Professional Trainer & Consultant
jsestak@pathway.net

How to Use this Text

What makes a good computer programming text? Sound pedagogy and the most current, complete materials. That is what you will find in the new *Java Programming Projects*. Not only will you find an inviting layout, but also many features to enhance learning.

Objectives— Objectives are listed at the beginning of each lesson, along with a suggested time for completion of the lesson. This allows you to look ahead to what you will be learning and to pace your work.

Program Code Examples—Many examples of program code are included in the text to illustrate concepts under discussion.

Projects—Projects present hands-on application of programming concepts and show the analysis, design, and implementation stages of the software development life cycle.

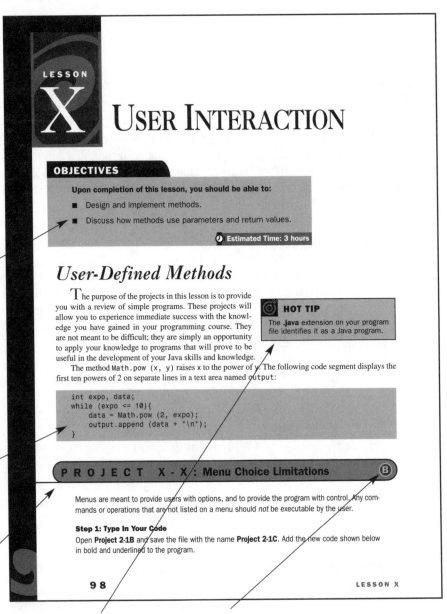

LESSON X

USER INTERACTION

OBJECTIVES

Upon completion of this lesson, you should be able to:

- Design and implement methods.
- Discuss how methods use parameters and return values.

⏱ **Estimated Time: 3 hours**

User-Defined Methods

The purpose of the projects in this lesson is to provide you with a review of simple programs. These projects will allow you to experience immediate success with the knowledge you have gained in your programming course. They are not meant to be difficult; they are simply an opportunity to apply your knowledge to programs that will prove to be useful in the development of your Java skills and knowledge.

The method Math.pow (x, y) raises x to the power of y. The following code segment displays the first ten powers of 2 on separate lines in a text area named output:

> **HOT TIP**
> The **.java** extension on your program file identifies it as a Java program.

```
int expo, data;
while (expo <= 10){
    data = Math.pow (2, expo);
    output.append (data + "\n");
}
```

PROJECT X - X: Menu Choice Limitations Ⓑ

Menus are meant to provide users with options, and to provide the program with control. Any commands or operations that are not listed on a menu should *not* be executable by the user.

Step 1: Type In Your Code

Open **Project 2-1B** and save the file with the name **Project 2-1C**. Add the new code shown below in bold and underlined to the program.

9 8

LESSON X

Hot Tip—These boxes provide enrichment information about Java.

Skill Level Icons— Each project and end-of-lesson activity is identified as either a beginner (B), intermediate (I), or advanced (A) level exercise.

How to Use this Text

Summary—At the end of each lesson, you will find a summary to help you complete the end-of-lesson activities.

Review Questions—Review material at the end of each lesson enables you to prepare for assessment of the content presented.

SCANS (Secretary's Commission on Achieving Necessary Skills)—The U.S. Department of Labor has identified the school-to-careers competencies. The five workplace competencies (resources, interpersonal skills, information, systems, and technology) and foundation skills (basic skills, thinking skills, and personal qualities) are identified in Projects and end-of-lesson activities throughout the text. More information on SCANS can be found on the *Electronic Instructor*.

Step 2: Add Your Code to the Event

If you were to "run" this program right now, you would have a decent-looking form that opened, accepted text into the "Enter Miles" box, and then did nothing—unless you maximized, minimized, or closed the form. VB is *event* driven

Summary

In this lesson, you learned:

■ The modern computer age began in the late 1940s with the development of ENIAC. Business computing became practical in the 1950s, and time-sharing computers advanced computing in large organizations in the 1960s.

LESSON X REVIEW QUESTIONS

WRITTEN QUESTIONS

Write your answers to the following questions.

1. What are the three major hardware components of a computer?
2. Name three input devices.

TESTING YOUR SKILLS

Estimated Time:
Application 1-1 30 minutes
Application 1-2 30 minutes
Application 1-3 30 minutes

APPLICATION X-X

1. Add code to Project 1-1 that converts kilometers into miles.
   a. Open the **Project 1-1** program file.
   b. After the code that creates the output of the miles to kilometers conversion, add the necessary lines to perform a kilometers to miles conversion. The lines of code should be similar to the code used for the original program.

      HINT: The conversion this time is going in reverse. Use your algebra skills!

   c. Save your revised program as **App1-1**.

CRITICAL THINKING Ⓐ

Estimated Time: 1 hour

You have an idea for a program that will help the local pizza shop handle take-out orders. Your friend suggests an interview with the shop's owner to discuss her user requirements before you get started on the program. Explain why this is a good suggestion, and list the questions you would ask the owner to help you determine the user requirements.

9 9

Testing Your Skills—End-of-lesson hands-on application of what has been learned in the lesson allows you to actually apply the techniques covered.

Critical Thinking Activity—Each lesson gives you an opportunity to apply creative analysis to situations presented.

CONTENTS

Try These Projects for More Programming Practice

Exciting new products from South-Western!

Our new programming activities workbooks offer additional projects that reinforce introductory instruction on Java, C++, and Visual Basic. These cover everything from beginning, to intermediate, to advanced topics to meet your programming needs.

- **NEW! Java Programming Projects, Activities Workbook** by CEP, Inc. and Sestak, has 10 lessons with 45 projects. Also, there are 22 applications exercises and 11 critical thinking projects. These projects number over 35 hours-of -instruction on the most widely used beginning through advanced features of Java.

Text, soft cover, 288 pages	0-538-69404-1
Electronic Instructor CD-ROM Package, 112 pages	0-538-69405-X

Other Companion Texts from South-Western:

- **Java Complete Course in Programming and Problem Solving** by Lambert and Osborne is the most comprehensive instructional text available for learning Java. It contains 75+ hours of instruction on the most widely used beginning through advanced features of Java. Covers Java for both Windows and Macintosh.

Student book, hard cover	0-538-68707-X
Student text-workbook/data CD-ROM package, soft spine cover	0-538-68708-8
Activities Workbook	0-538-68710-X
Electronic Instructor CD-ROM Package	0-538-68709-6

- **Java: Introduction to Programming** by Knowlton covers the beginning through intermediate features of Java in 35+ hours of instruction. The text is available in hard or soft cover and is for the Windows version of Java only.

Student book, hard cover	0-538-68565-4
Student book/3.5" template disk package, soft spine cover	0-538-68772-X
Activities Workbook	0-538-68571-9
Electronic Instructor CD-ROM Package	0-538-68557-3

- **NEW! C++ Programming Projects, Activities Workbook** by CEP, Inc. and Sestak, has 10 lessons with 30 projects. Also, there are 18 applications exercises and 11 critical thinking projects. These projects number over 35 hours-of -instruction on the most widely used beginning through advanced features of C++.

Text, soft cover, 272 pages	0-538-69081-X
Electronic Instructor CD-ROM Package, 96 pages	0-538-69082-8

- **NEW! Microsoft Visual Basic Programming Projects, Activities Workbook** by CEP, Inc. and Sestak, has 10 lessons with 30 projects. Also, there are 18 applications exercises and 11 critical thinking projects. These projects number over 35 hours-of -instruction on the most widely used beginning through advanced features of Visual Basic.

Text, soft cover, 272 pages	0-538-68894-7
Electronic Instructor CD-ROM Package, 96 pages	0-538-68895-5

A new feature available for these products is the Electronic Instructor, which includes a printed Instructors manual and a CD-ROM. The CD-ROM contains tests, lesson plans, all solutions files, and more! Also, ask about our ProgramPaks for compiler software bundles!

Join Us On the Internet
www.swep.com

South-Western
EDUCATIONAL PUBLISHING
Thomson Learning™

List of Projects

APPLETS AND SIMPLE PROGRAMS

Copying/scanning is not permitted and may be a violation of copyright laws.
© 2001 by South-Western Educational Publishing.

OBJECTIVES

On completion of this lesson, you should be able to:

- Explain Java applets.
- Describe the parts of a Java applet.
- Explain the process of applet development.
- Demonstrate your understanding of Java.
- Produce working applets from the instructions provided.
- Practice the concepts learned in your programming course.

⏱ **Estimated Time: 2 hours**

Introduction

The purpose of the projects in this lesson is to provide you with a review of simple applets. These projects will allow you to experience immediate success with the knowledge you have gained in your programming course. The projects in this lesson are not meant to be difficult; we are simply giving you the opportunity to apply your knowledge to programs that will prove to be useful in the development of your Java skills.

The other, equally important, purpose of these projects is to allow you to have *fun!* Programming should not always be serious business. That will happen when someone is giving you a paycheck. Programming should be something that you enjoy and anticipate!

This lesson presents a few simple applets that will focus on the following:

- **Understandng Java applets.** Java applets are programs that run within *Web browsers*. They consist of one or more *classes,* and they themselves can be thought of as a class. Java applets contain *data members* and *methods*. The major difference between Java and its parent language, C++, is that Java expects you to use existing classes. Java applets need to be "contained" within an *HTML* (HyperText Markup Language) page in order to execute. The only way that you can be sure that applets will run on your browser is to use a Java *plug-in* or an *ActiveX* component.

- **Learning the parts of a Java applet.** Java applets begin with *Import* statements. The Import statements make sure that the *class library packages* needed to allow the applet to build on existing classes, and to compile/interpret the applet, are included. The applet then begins a *class*

1

definition. An applet must contain at least one class, and the name of the class *must* be the same name as the file in which it is saved. The class itself will contain data members and methods. ***Extends*** is probably the most important keyword in Java. Classes are not created from scratch in Java; they ***inherit*** from existing classes. Once your class is "extended," your applet is almost ready to run.

■ **Grasping the process of applet development.** Once the applet is created, it *must* be saved in a file that has *exactly the same name* as the class in the applet. The file also must end with the *.java* extension. Once the class is complete, it must be compiled. The resulting bytecodes from the compile are stored in a file with a *.class* extension. The path to the compiled .class file is then inserted into an HTML page in order to execute. You should test your applet in an ***applet viewer***, although some compilers, like Microsoft J++, allow you to test the applet in your system's browser. As long as you have a text file with the .java extension you should be able to run your applet within any of the more popular Java compilers.

■ **Demonstrating your understanding of Java.** Anyone can talk a good game, but if you have working programs to show people, especially potential employers, that carries a great deal more weight than simply using buzzwords. This book will help you develop a better understanding of Java by reinforcing the practical with a healthy dose of theory through short-answer questions and explanations. In addition, it will help you become more familiar with the Java class libraries/document set. All the core API specifications are found here. The book is set up so that you can write down code and answer questions directly on the pages on which you are working. For that reason and others, this book will become a valuable resource for you.

■ **Producing working applets from the instructions provided and practicing the concepts learned in your programming course.** Each lesson is aimed at making you productive. As we previously mentioned, this gives you a working demonstration of your abilities. It also gives you a chance to expand on the lessons learned in your programming class. Combined, these lessons will allow you to expand your abilities.

So, settle in, get ready to work, and prepare to learn one of the most exciting languages in use today!

PROJECT 1-1: Distance Conversions (B)

This applet will perform the conversion of U.S. distance measurements to metric measurements. This conversion applet could be useful to distance runners in converting their runs from miles to kilometers.

Step 1: Start Your Compiler

The projects in this book have been developed using the Microsoft J++ 6.0 compiler, the Sun Java–compliant version (Visual Studio 6.0 Service Pack 2). The figures show screens from that development environment; however, the programs you will be writing will work whether you are using a simple text editor, Visual J++ 6.0, Borland's JBuilder, or Sun Java.

Figure 1-1 shows the Visual J++ opening screen. The gray "pane" to the left is the Editor area. This is the area in which you will be writing the code. It functions just like a text editor.

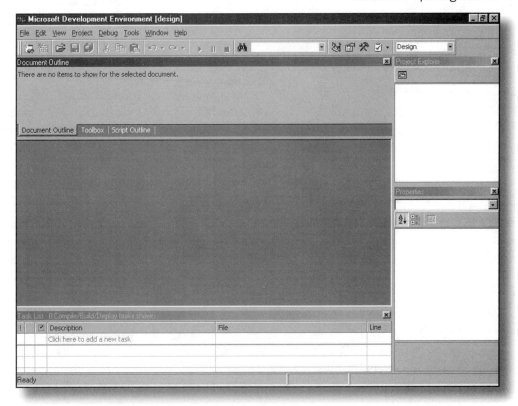

Now that you've started your compiler, you can begin typing in code.

Step 2: Type in Your Code

Type in the code as follows:

```java
import java.awt.*;
import java.applet.*;
import java.awt.event.*;

public class Proj1_1 extends Applet implements ActionListener
{
    double MI, KM;
    Label prompt;
    TextField input;

    public void init()
    {
        prompt = new Label ("Enter the number of miles you've run: ");
        add(prompt);

        input = new TextField(5);
        add(input);

        input.addActionListener(this);
    }
```

```
public void actionPerformed (ActionEvent e)
{
        MI = Integer.parseInt(input.getText());
        KM = MI / .62;
        repaint();
}

public void paint (Graphics g)
{
        g.drawString ("You have run " + KM + " kilometers.", 70, 75);
}
}
```

Step 3: Save Your Program

Since this is a short, simple program, it wouldn't be too disastrous if you lost your work before saving it. However, in practice it makes good sense to save your programs early and often. Ideally, you should save after every four or five lines of code. This way if something should happen you would not need to retype a great deal of code. Plus it gives you a chance to pause and review your code.

Save your program with the name **Proj1_1**. Your compiler will not compile the applet unless it is saved with exactly the same name as the name of the class within your applet. If your compiler does not automatically place the .java extension on your file, you must save the file after adding the extension to identify it as a Java program.

Step 4: Review Your Code

To test your understanding of program components, answer the following questions in the space provided.

1. Explain the import statements.

   _____

   _____

   _____

   _____

   _____

2. Explain why there is no main().

   _____

   _____

   _____

   _____

   _____

 HOT TIP

The .java extension on your program file identifies it as a Java program. Compiled Java programs are identified with a .class extension. The compiled .class file is the file that must be placed within your HTML page.

 HOT TIP

Familiarize yourself with the extensions that your compiler assigns to your Java files. For example, Microsoft J++ Version 6.0 saves with .jav and .cla extensions.

 HOT TIP

In practice you should always save your programs with meaningful filenames. A file named **MI to KM** means more to someone using your program than a file named **Proj1_1**.

 HOT TIP

Make sure your compiler is Sun Java–compliant. Sun Java is the standard for this programming language. This means that Microsoft J++ 6.0 must have the Visual Studio 6.0 Service Pack 2 installed.

3. What are the { } used for?

_____

_____

_____

4. Explain the *extends* keyword.

_____

_____

_____

5. Explain the *implements* keyword.

_____

_____

_____

6. What are MI and KM? What is the significance of *double?*

_____

_____

_____

7. Explain primitive data types.

_____

_____

_____

8. Explain Label and TextField.

_____

_____

_____

9. Explain the `init()`.

_____

_____

_____

10. Explain the `add()`.

_____

_____

_____

11. What is the significance of the semicolons?

_____

_____

_____

12. Explain the `actionPerformed()`.

_____

_____

_____

13. Explain `Integer.parseInt()`.

_____

_____

_____

14. Explain the `getText()`.

_____

_____

_____

15. Explain the `paint()`.

_____

_____

_____

16. Explain the `drawString()`.

_____

_____

_____

Reviewing the correct answers to the above questions with your teacher and class will provide you with an overview of the basic components of a Java program. It's important to know exactly what is happening in your program so that you are able to correct any errors.

Step 5: Compile and Run

Enter the commands necessary to compile and run your program. If you are running Visual J++ 6.0, simply click the **Run** button. Your applet will begin to compile. If there are no errors, your applet should run within the Microsoft Applet Viewer. If any errors occur during the compile process, check your code, correct any errors, and rerun the program.

 HOT TIP

Applets should always be tested in the applet viewer. Completed projects can be executed within your browser.

If you are not using Visual J++ 6.0 as your compiler, check with your teacher as to the appropriate commands to use to compile and run under your compiler. List the name of your compiler and the appropriate commands below:

Your compiler: _____

Run command: _____

Remember to save your program any time you make changes!

Step 6: Add Comments to Your Code

The biggest complaint you will hear from any programmer, especially those doing maintenance or modification programming, is the lack of documentation included in programs. You should make it a habit to add comments to your code so that you, and those who follow, will have some idea about what's going on in your program.

When should you add comments? Most programmers add them before they begin working on a section or after the fact. The easiest way is to add comments as you are writing the program. This gives you a better idea of what each section is supposed to do and it assists in the organization of the program. It also helps you remember what it is that you coded.

Add the following comments, shown in italics, to your program code:

```java
// These are the classes needed for this applet to execute.

import java.awt.*;
import java.applet.*;
import java.awt.event.*;

// You are extending the Applet class into your Proj1_1 class.

public class Proj1_1 extends Applet implements ActionListener
{

    // These are the data members of your class.
    // The doubles are primitive data types, the other a Label, the
    // third a TextField.
    double MI, KM;
    Label prompt;
    TextField input;


    // This method will perform what you need done as your Applet
    // initializes.
    public void init()
    {
        // This creates and places a new Label in your applet.
        prompt = new Label ("Enter the number of miles you've run: ");
        add(prompt);

        // This creates and places a new TextField in your applet.
        input = new TextField(5);
```

```
        add(input);

        // This starts your applet listening for action regarding the
        // TextField.
        input.addActionListener(this);
    }

    // This method describes what actions will be performed by this
    // class.

    public void actionPerformed (ActionEvent e)
    {
        MI = Integer.parseInt(input.getText());
        KM = MI / .62;
        repaint();
    }

    // This method "paints" a message within your applet.

    public void paint (Graphics g)
    {
        g.drawString ("You have run " + KM + " kilometers.", 70, 75);
    }
}
```

Answer the following questions regarding the comments added to your code:

1. Explain why the comments were added.

_____

_____

_____

2. Explain why the comments were added in these specific places in the code.

_____

_____

_____

3. Would you have added comments in any other area? Why?

_____

_____

_____

4. Would you have modified the comments in any way? Why?

_____

_____

_____

5. In your opinion, are the comments self-explanatory? Explain.

_____

_____

_____

Step 7: Compile and Run Your Program

Changes you make to a program, such as adding comments, can cause the program to not run properly. Any time you make changes to your program, you need to recompile it.

Enter the commands necessary to compile and run your program. If you are running Visual J++ 6.0, simply click the **Run** button. Your applet will begin to compile. If there are no errors, your applet should run within the Microsoft Applet Viewer. If errors occur during the compile process, check your code, correct any errors, and re-run the program. Remember that it is entirely possible that even a simple program like this can show errors if it is not typed in properly.

If you need to review the commands necessary to compile and run under your compiler, see Step 5 above.

Congratulations! You have successfully completed your first simple applet. The output should look similar to Figure 1-2.

FIGURE 1-2
Proj1_1 applet

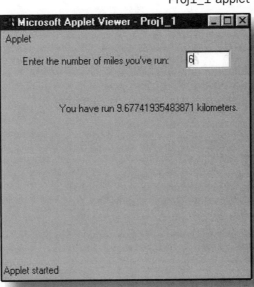

The next applet you write will perform the calculation done on a monthly checking account statement. This calculation takes the balance that the bank says is in your account, adds any deposits not recorded by the bank, subtracts checks not recorded by the bank, and provides you with an adjusted bank balance that should be equal to the amount in your checkbook. Obviously, this calculation can easily be performed on a calculator; however, it is good practice for you to request information to be input to the program from a user.

With most of the easy programs you have written and run in your programming classes, *you* have probably provided the necessary values to make the program run by coding the data into your program. This is not the way it works when you really begin to write programs. You create an interface that requests information from the user and then your program works magic with the user's data!

One thing to keep in mind in these early lessons is that your Java applets may not seem overly organized. That's OK! The organization and structured layouts will come as you progress through this book.

Step 1: Start Your Compiler

If your compiler is not already running, start it now.

Step 2: Type in Your Code

This time, let's type in the comments as we are typing in the code. As you can see by reviewing the code below, there are no comments. It's your job to insert the appropriate comments where necessary. Save the program as **Proj1_2**. Make sure you include the **.java** extension if your compiler does not do it for you. *REMEMBER:* While you are typing the code, save your program regularly.

```java
import java.awt.*;
import java.applet.*;
import java.awt.event.*;

public class Proj1_2 extends Applet implements ActionListener
{
    Label pmtBankBal, pmtOutDep, pmtOutChecks;
    TextField txtBankBal, txtOutDep, txtOutChecks;
    int intBal, intDep, intChecks;
    Float fltBal, fltDep, fltChecks;
    float fltAdjBal;

    public void init()
    {
        pmtBankBal = new Label("Enter the Bank Balance: ");
        add(pmtBankBal);

        txtBankBal = new TextField(10);
        add(txtBankBal);

        pmtOutDep = new Label("Enter Outstanding Deposits: ");
```

```
            add(pmtOutDep);

            txtOutDep = new TextField(10);
            add(txtOutDep);

            pmtOutChecks = new Label("Enter Outstanding Checks: ");
            add(pmtOutChecks);

            txtOutChecks = new TextField(10);
            add(txtOutChecks);
            txtOutChecks.addActionListener(this);

    }

    public void actionPerformed(ActionEvent e)
    {
            fltBal = Float.valueOf(txtBankBal.getText());
            fltDep = Float.valueOf(txtOutDep.getText());
            fltChecks = Float.valueOf(txtOutChecks.getText());
            fltAdjBal = (fltBal.floatValue()  + fltDep.floatValue()) -
                fltChecks.floatValue();
            repaint();
    }

    public void paint(Graphics g)
    {
            g.drawString("Your adjusted bank balance is " + fltAdjBal, 100,
                135);
    }

}
```

Answer the following questions regarding the comments added to your code:

1. Explain what comments you added to your code.

_____

_____

_____

2. Explain where your comments were added. Why?

_____

_____

_____

3. Are there any areas in which you did not add comments? Why?

_____

_____

_____

4. In reviewing your comments, would you have modified them in any way? Why?

_____

_____

_____

5. In your opinion, are your comments self-explanatory? Explain.

_____

_____

_____

Step 3: Save Your Program

When you have finished typing the code, save your program once more before moving on to the next step. This way if anything happens, you will not be forced to retype any of the code.

Step 4: Compile and Run

Enter the commands necessary to compile and run your program. If you are running Visual J++ 6.0, simply click the **Run** button. Your applet will begin to compile. If there are no errors, your applet should run within the Microsoft Applet Viewer. If errors occur during the compile process, check your code, correct any errors, and rerun the program.

Remember to save your program any time you make changes!

If you have typed the code correctly, you should now have a second operating program. Congratulations!

Summary

In this lesson, you wrote two Java applets. You should have noticed that neither applet contains a main function, and that each is run within an applet viewer or can be run within an HTML page in a browser.

With each applet you have imported the classes needed to allow the applet to execute. And by extending a specific class you have begun to practice inheritance, which will be explained as you progress through this book. You saved your Java files, and then compiled and ran them within the applet viewer.

You have also reviewed the four steps of program development. If you compare the first program to the second, you will see that it included a total of seven steps versus only four in the second project. The four steps presented in the second project actually represent the four steps of program development: write, compile, link, and execute.

We all know that programming is not easy. Programming involves problem-solving skills that need to be utilized when our programs do not run or do not run correctly. Understanding the program development cycle is only part of the solution. You have to develop a solid understanding of the language in which you are programming.

Beginning with the next lesson, you will be required to provide more input on each project. Remember, the projects presented for you to complete will develop and enhance your Java skills and knowledge. The fun is only beginning!

LESSON 1 REVIEW QUESTIONS

SHORT ANSWER

Define the following in the space provided.

1. Compiler

   _____

   _____

2. Text editor

   _____

3. Program development

   _____

4. .java extension

   _____

5. Comments

   _____

   _____

6. Compile

   _____

7. .class extension

   _____

8. Run

   _____

9. Execute

   _____

10. Primitive data types

    _____

    _____

11. Web browser

_____

_____

12. Classes

_____

_____

13. Instance variables

_____

_____

14. Methods

_____

_____

15. HTML

_____

_____

16. ActiveX

_____

_____

_____

_____

17. Plug-ins

_____

_____

18. Inheritance

_____

_____

19. Applet viewer

_____

_____

_____

20. Extends

_____

_____

_____

_____

21. Import

_____

_____

WRITTEN QUESTIONS

Write your answers to the following questions in the space provided.

1. Why should you save your work early and often?

_____

_____

2. Explain the significance of including comments in your code.

_____

_____

3. Identify and explain the main sections of a Java applet.

_____

_____

_____

_____

_____

4. Discuss some of the more common errors that you have found when debugging programs you have written.

_____

_____

_____

5. Discuss the importance of the _extends_ keyword.

_____

_____

_____

_____

6. Explain the process of writing, saving, compiling, testing, and then running a Java applet within a browser.

_____

_____

_____

_____

_____

_____

_____

_____

TESTING YOUR SKILLS

Estimated Time:
Application 1-1 1 hour
Application 1-2 45 minutes

APPLICATION 1-1

1. Add code to Proj1_1.java that converts kilometers into miles.
  a. Open the **Proj1_1.java** program file.
  b. After the code that creates the output of the miles-to-kilometers conversion to the screen, add the necessary lines to perform a kilometers-to-miles conversion. The lines of code should be similar to the code used for the original program. The applet should respond to action on either TextField. (*HINT:* The conversion this time is going in reverse. Use your algebra skills!)

2. Save your revised program as **App1_1.java**.

APPLICATION 1-2 B

1. Explain each line of code in Proj1_2.java.
  a. Open **Proj1_2.java**.
  b. On each line below, write a short explanation for the corresponding line of code. Remember that the lines of code in a Java program are not numbered. You will need to count each line beginning with the very first line of the program. (*Hint:* Comment lines and blank lines also count as a line of code.)

  1. _____
  2. _____
  3. _____
  4. _____
  5. _____
  6. _____
  7. _____

8. _____
9. _____
10. _____
11. _____
12. _____
13. _____
14. _____
15. _____
16. _____
17. _____
18. _____
19. _____
20. _____
21. _____
22. _____
23. _____
24. _____
25. _____
26. _____
27. _____
28. _____
29. _____
30. _____
31. _____
32. _____
33. _____
34. _____
35. _____
36. _____
37. _____
38. _____
39. _____
40. _____
41. _____
42. _____
43. _____
44. _____
45. _____
46. _____
47. _____
48. _____
49. _____
50. _____

CANS

Write an applet, similar to Project 1-1, that converts Fahrenheit temperature to Celsius and back again.

USER INTERACTION

Introduction

In programming, ***user interaction*** simply means that the user is enabled to control certain aspects of a program. Every computer program is written for someone. Who that someone is and what they need the program to do for them is a very important part of program design. You, as the programmer, need to identify these ***end users*** and gather information from them. The information you gather not only provides you with valuable information about the coding of the program, but it also gives you an idea of how the program should be presented in order to make it user-friendly.

In general, programs do only a few things: they gather information from the user, process information, output information, and store information. The specifics of each of these functions depend on the needs of the user. Although a program performs some functions "behind the scenes," without the involvement of the user, most programs require the user to exercise some control over their operations. That is, the user must interact with the program in order to get from it what he or she needs. The starting point for this interaction, as well as providing control limitations, is the ***user interface***.

The user interface can be as simple as a text menu, or it can be an elaborate design of menu bars, text fields, buttons, check boxes, choice, and other graphical user interface (GUI) objects found in most of the software used today. Regardless, the function is the same: to gather information from the user so that the program can perform the operations required by the user. The user interface is also the mechanism through which control of programming operations is determined. If there is *not* a menu option for a specific procedure, the user cannot choose to perform that procedure. This leaves control in the "hands" of the program. As you can see, user interaction is an important part of programming.

This lesson will focus on the following:

■ **Learning about user interaction.** The topics discussed in this introduction will be reinforced throughout the lesson. User interaction is a key part of programming and needs to become second nature.

■ **Understanding the reasons for user interaction.** As you code your applets, each step will be explained thoroughly so that you will understand the significance. In addition, the user-friendly concept of a program will be continually addressed. You hear a lot of talk about the "user-friend-liness" of a program. If you design an *intuitive* interface, this will only increase the friendliness of your program.

■ **Designing interfaces for user interaction.** Each of the projects in this lesson will result in a completed interface. However, the underlying functionality may not be included because the focus will be on using GUI components and design. You will concentrate on user input and program output. You will also touch on *aesthetics*—a term used when talking about the attractiveness and common sense of the interface design. Remember that you are only at the beginning of this project book and some of the more advanced structuring features will not be introduced until later.

■ **Integrating checks into your user interfaces.** There will be times when users will need to verify the actions they have performed or have chosen to perform. For example, when deciding to delete a file, users are usually prompted with a *confirm* question. This question is usually, "Are you sure you want to do this?" You will learn about checks that should be built into interfaces.

■ **Producing working applications from the instructions provided.** You will code working applications in every lesson in this book. There is no better way to learn how to program than to program!

So, strap yourself in, get ready to work, and prepare to have fun!

PROJECT 2-1: Menu Choices

In Lesson 1, your projects used simple interfaces. For example, in Project 1-1 you simply asked the user to input the number of miles run, and in Project 1-2 you asked the user to input three predetermined values.

Now you will create an interface that provides users with a method through which they can input data into the program. You will begin with a simple interface and modify it to include the controls mentioned in the Introduction.

Step 1: Start Your Compiler

If your compiler is not already running, start it now.

Step 2: Type in Your Code

Type your code exactly as shown below. Save this program with the name **Proj2_1.java**. Remember to save your work often as you type.

```
// Proj2_1.java
// Menu Choices


// The base classes from which your applet inherits
```

```java
import java.awt.*;
import java.applet.*;
import java.awt.event.*;

// Your class definition - it extends applet
// and will "listen" for an action
public class Proj2_1 extends Applet implements ActionListener
{

    // Your member variables
    Label choice1, choice2, choice3, choice4, choice5, prompt1;
    TextField selection;

    // Remember that an int is a primitive data type
    int number;

    // This method contains the things that happen when your applet
    // initializes
    public void init()
    {

        // You add 6 new labels and one new text field to your applet
        choice1 = new Label("1 - Enter A New Record.");
        add(choice1);

        choice2 = new Label("2 - Modify An Existing Record.");
        add(choice2);

        choice3 = new Label("3 - Delete An Existing Record.");
        add(choice3);

        choice4 = new Label("4 - View/Print An Existing Record.");
        add(choice4);

        choice5 = new Label("5 - Exit");
        add(choice5);

        prompt1 = new Label("    Enter Your Choice: ");
        add(prompt1);

        selection = new TextField(3);
        add(selection);
        selection.addActionListener(this);
    }

    // When data is entered into the text field and the enter key is pressed
    // the actions in this method are performed
    public void actionPerformed(ActionEvent e)
    {
        number = Integer.parseInt(selection.getText());
        repaint();
    }
```

```
// This paint method displays "text strings" on your applet
// depending on the choice the user makes
public void paint(Graphics g)
{
        if (number == 1)
                g.drawString("You chose to add a record.", 70, 150);
        if (number == 2)
                g.drawString("You chose to modify a record.", 70, 150);
        if (number == 3)
                g.drawString("You chose to delete a record.", 70, 150);
        if (number == 4)
                g.drawString("You chose to view/print a record.", 70,
                150);
        if (number == 5)
                g.drawString("Close the browser window to stop
                execution!", 70, 150);
}
}
```

Step 3: Review Your Code

To test your understanding of the program components, answer the following questions in the space provided.

1. Explain the import statements.

_____

_____

2. Explain why there is no main().

_____

3. What are the { } used for?

_____

4. Explain `Label` and `TextField`.

_____

5. What is the significance of `int`?

_____

_____

6. What is the significance of the semicolons?

_____

7. Explain the init() method.

_____

8. Explain the following line of code: `choice1 = new Label("1 - Enter A New Record.");`

_____

_____

9. Explain the add() method.

_____

_____

10. What is the purpose of the order of the add()?

_____

_____

11. Explain the following line of code: `selection.addActionListener(this);`

_____

_____

12. Explain the actionPerformed() method.

_____

_____

13. Explain the two lines of code in the body of the actionPerformed().

_____

_____

14. Explain the paint() method.

_____

_____

15. Explain one of the if statements contained in the body of the paint().

_____

_____

Reviewing the correct answers to the above questions with your teacher and class will provide you with an overview of the basic components of a Java applet. It's important to know exactly what is happening in your program so that you are able to correct any errors that occur.

Step 4: Compile and Run

Enter the commands necessary to compile and run your program. If you are running Visual J++ 6.0, simply click the **Run** button. Your applet will begin to compile. If there are no errors, your applet should run within the Microsoft Applet Viewer. If errors occur during the compile process, check your code, correct any errors, and rerun the program.

If you are not using Visual J++ 6.0 as your compiler, check with your teacher as to the appropriate commands to use to compile and run under your compiler. List the name of your compiler and the appropriate commands below:

Your compiler: _____

Run command: _____

HOT TIP

Applets should always be tested in the Applet Viewer. Completed projects can be executed within your browser.

HOT TIP

A single HTML page can be used repeatedly to execute your completed applets. You only need to change the name of the .class file that the HTML page calls.

Remember to save your program any time you make changes!

Step 5: Review Your Output

Your output should look like that shown in Figure 2-1.

FIGURE 2-1
Proj2_1 applet viewer

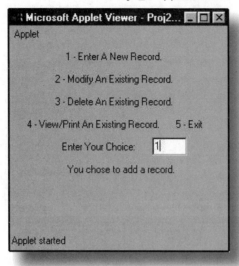

Answer the following questions regarding the output:

1. Why do the buttons and the output move around depending on the size of the applet window?

_____

_____

2. What can be done to separate and organize the output to some degree?

_____

_____

3. Explain the drawString method.

_____

_____

4. Why should we organize the output to the screen?

_____

_____

By using different GUI components, you can arrange the output to the screen. In the next project you will create the same menu you just finished—only this time it will contain buttons.

PROJECT 2-2 : Menu Buttons   Ⓑ

This program will build on the program you completed in Project 2-1. Now that you have your menu, and it looks good, you will make it even better!

What is this menu to be used for? For what program, and for what purpose? From reading the menu you know it deals with file manipulations, but you need to know more. The simple menu, at this point, can be used for *any* program, since all programs usually incorporate these commands. That's one of the reasons you'll be keeping this file, so you can reuse it with other programs. But you need to make this menu more specific so that it is appropriate for the program you are writing.

Step 1: Start Your Compiler

If your compiler is not already running, start it now.

Step 2: Type in Your Code

Type in the code as shown below. Save the program as **Proj2_2.java**. Make sure you include the **.java** extension. **REMEMBER:** Save your program regularly as you type the code.

```
// Proj2_2

// The classes from which your class will inherit
import java.awt.*;
import java.applet.*;
import java.awt.event.*;


// Your class definition
public class Proj2_2 extends Applet
{
   // the button variables your program will use
   Button choice1, choice2, choice3, choice4, choice5;

   // the initialization procedure for your applet
   public void init()
   {
   // Adding each of the buttons and
   // adding an action listener to each one
   choice1 = new Button("Add New Record");
   choice1.addActionListener(new choice1Handler(this));
   add(choice1);

   choice2 = new Button("Modify Record");
   choice2.addActionListener(new choice2Handler(this));
   add(choice2);

   choice3 = new Button("Delete Record");
   choice3.addActionListener(new choice3Handler(this));
   add(choice3);

   choice4 = new Button("View/Print Record");
```

```
    choice4.addActionListener(new choice4Handler(this));
    add(choice4);

    choice5 = new Button("Exit");
    choice5.addActionListener(new choice5Handler(this));
    add(choice5);


    }


// Each button will use a separate class method to listen for
// a click on that specific button
class choice1Handler implements ActionListener {
    Applet applet;

    public choice1Handler (Applet Proj2_2) {applet = Proj2_2;}
    public void actionPerformed(ActionEvent e)
    {
        applet.showStatus("You chose to add a new record.");
    }
}

class choice2Handler implements ActionListener {
    Applet applet;

    public choice2Handler (Applet Proj2_2) {applet = Proj2_2;}

    public void actionPerformed(ActionEvent e)
    {
        applet.showStatus("You chose to modify an existing record.");
    }
}

class choice3Handler implements ActionListener {
    Applet applet;

    public choice3Handler (Applet Proj2_2) {applet = Proj2_2;}

    public void actionPerformed(ActionEvent e)
    {
        applet.showStatus("You chose to delete an existing record.");
    }
}

class choice4Handler implements ActionListener {
    Applet applet;

    public choice4Handler (Applet Proj2_2) {applet = Proj2_2;}

    public void actionPerformed(ActionEvent e)
    {
        applet.showStatus("You chose to view/print an existing record.");
```

```
      }
  }

class choice5Handler implements ActionListener {
   Applet applet;

   public choice5Handler (Applet Proj2_2) {applet = Proj2_2;}

   public void actionPerformed(ActionEvent e)
   {
         applet.showStatus("Close the browser to halt execution of this
applet!!");
   }
}
```

Answer the following questions regarding the above code:

1. Explain what each of the button components will do.

_____

_____

_____

_____

2. Explain, in general, what the choiceXHandlers will do.

_____

_____

_____

3. Explain the following line of code:

```
choice3.addActionListener(new choice3Handler(this));
```

_____

_____

4. Explain the following block of code:

```
class choice1Handler implements ActionListener {
   Applet applet;

   public choice1Handler (Applet Proj2_2) {applet = Proj2_2;}
   public void actionPerformed(ActionEvent e)
   {
         applet.showStatus("You chose to add a new record.");
   }
}
```

_____

_____

_____

_____

Step 3: Save Your Program

When you have finished typing the code, save your program once more before moving on to the next step.

Step 4: Compile and Run

Enter the commands necessary to compile and run your program. If errors occur during any part of this process, check your code, correct any errors, and recompile the program.

Remember to save your program any time you make changes!

If you have typed the code correctly, you should now have an enhanced applet that looks something like Figure 2-2.

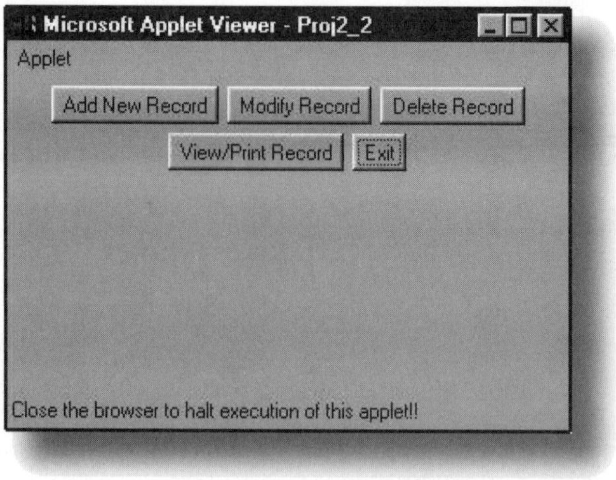

Congratulations! You now have an enhanced menu that looks neat and organized!

FIGURE 2-2
Proj2_2 Applet Viewer

PROJECT 2-3 : Menu Aesthetics—GridLayout

There is one last item to take care of in regard to menus. You are going to use one of the *layout managers* included with Java. The layout managers are provided to arrange components for design/presentation purposes. The layout managers *inherit* from class *objects* and implement the layout manager *interface*. The interface defines the methods that a layout manager can use.

You will use the GridLayout layout manager to organize your menu. You will be able to designate the number of rows and columns to be used as well as the spacing between each of the components you use.

Menus are meant to provide users with options, and to provide the program with control. Any commands or operations that are *not* listed on a menu should *not* be executable by the user.

Again, the underlying functionality will not be provided here, but will be presented in upcoming lessons.

Step 1: Start Your Compiler

If your compiler is not already running, start it now.

Step 2: Type in Your Code

Open **Proj2_2** and save the file with the name **Proj2_3.java**. Add the new code shown below in bold and underlined to the program. In addition, you *must* change the class name *and* each reference to Proj2_2 from Proj2_2 to **Proj2_3**.

```
public class Proj2_3 extends Applet
{
// The button variables your applet will use
Button choice1, choice2, choice3, choice4, choice5;
```

```
public void init()
{
// The code needed to use GridLayout
setLayout (new GridLayout(5, 1, 5, 5));

class choice1Handler implements ActionListener {
Applet applet;

public choice1Handler (Applet Proj2_3) {applet = Proj2_3;}

class choice2Handler implements ActionListener {
Applet applet;

public choice2Handler (Applet Proj2_3) {applet = Proj2_3;}

class choice3Handler implements ActionListener {
Applet applet;

public choice3Handler (Applet Proj2_3) {applet = Proj2_3;}

class choice4Handler implements ActionListener {
Applet applet;

public choice4Handler (Applet Proj2_3) {applet = Proj2_3;}

class choice5Handler implements ActionListener {
Applet applet;

public choice5Handler (Applet Proj2_3) {applet = Proj2_3;}
```

Step 3: Save Your Program

When you have finished typing the code, save your program once more before moving on to the next step.

Step 4: Compile and Run

Enter the commands necessary to compile and run your program. If errors occur during any part of this process, check your code, correct any errors, and recompile the program.

Remember to save your program any time you make changes!

If you have typed the code correctly, you should now have an enhanced applet that looks something like Figure 2-3.

FIGURE 2-3
Proj2_3 applet viewer

Users will also require interfaces through which they enter data in the program. Menus are one simple way of enabling the user to make choices, but as you know, a program often needs more information from the user, and making a simple menu choice just won't suffice. For example, a database program may require the user to provide names, addresses, telephone numbers, e-mail addresses, Web sites, and maybe even pictures and sound files. The database programmer must create a way for the user to input such information in the program. This project focuses on the design and coding of a data input interface.

Step 1: Start Your Compiler

If your compiler is not already running, start it now.

Step 2: Type in Your Code

Type in the code as shown below. Save the program as **Proj2_4.java**. *REMEMBER:* Save often as you type in the code.

```java
// Proj2_4.java

import java.awt.*;
import java.applet.*;
import java.awt.event.*;


// Your class definition
public class Proj2_4 extends Applet implements ActionListener {

    // Four label and three text field components are used
    Label prompt1, prompt2, prompt3, result;
    TextField fname, lname, email;

    // Set up the initialization method
    public void init()
    {
        // This creates the grid layout
        setLayout (new GridLayout(4, 2, 5, 5));

        prompt1 = new Label("Enter first name");
        add(prompt1);

        fname = new TextField(20);
        add(fname);

        prompt2 = new Label("Enter last name");
        add(prompt2);

        lname = new TextField(20);
        add(lname);
```

```
        prompt3 = new Label("Enter E-Mail");
        add(prompt3);

        email = new TextField(20);
        add(email);
        email.addActionListener(this);

        result = new Label("");
        add(result);
    }


    // This sets the text property of the result label
    // for display purposes
    public void actionPerformed(ActionEvent e)
    {
        result.setText("You entered " + fname.getText() + " " +
lname.getText() + " " + email.getText() + ".");
    }
}
```

Step 3: Save Your Program

When you have finished typing the code, save your program once more before moving on to the next step.

Step 4: Compile and Run

Enter the commands necessary to compile and run your program. If errors occur during any part of this process, check your code, correct any errors, and recompile the program.

Remember to save your program any time you make changes!

If you have typed the code correctly, you should now have an enhanced applet that looks something like Figure 2-4.

FIGURE 2-4
Proj2_4 applet viewer

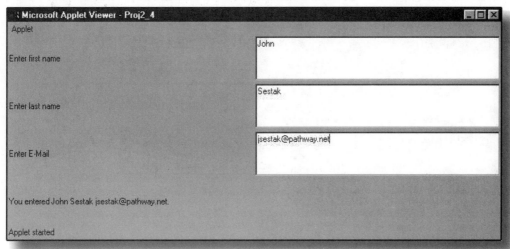

3 1

You need to be aware of a few things regarding this program: Error-checking is *not* being performed; therefore, you can enter anything into any field and it will be accepted. If you press the Enter key without entering a value, the program will not respond to anything *except* the Enter key. Otherwise, the program should work. **REMEMBER:** you are designing an interface, not coding a working menu. The "guts" of the menu will come in later lessons.

Building **objects**, or program components, like these is actually referred to as **object-oriented programming**. We are building components that can be reused in other programs.

Step 5: Explain Your Program

Explain each line or block of code in the program in the space provided below.

```
// Proj2_4.java
```


```
import java.awt.*;
import java.applet.*;
import java.awt.event.*;
```


```
// Your class definition
public class Proj2_4 extends Applet implements ActionListener {
```


```
// Four label and three text field components are used
Label prompt1, prompt2, prompt3, result;
TextField fname, lname, email;
```



```
// Set up the initialization method
public void init()
{
    // This creates the grid layout
    setLayout (new GridLayout(4, 2, 5, 5));

    prompt1 = new Label("Enter first name");
    add(prompt1);
```



```
fname = new TextField(20);
add(fname);
```

_____

_____

```
prompt2 = new Label("Enter last name");
add(prompt2);
```

_____

_____

```
lname = new TextField(20);
add(lname);
```

_____

_____

```
prompt3 = new Label("Enter E-Mail");
add(prompt3);
```

_____

_____

```
email = new TextField(20);
add(email);
email.addActionListener(this);
```

_____

_____

_____

```
    result = new Label("");
    add(result);
}
```

_____

_____

_____

```
// This sets the text property of the result label
// for display purposes
public void actionPerformed(ActionEvent e)
{
    result.setText("You entered " + fname.getText() + " " +
lname.getText() + " " + email.getText() + ".");
}
}
```

_____

_____

_____

_____

_____

Additional Methods

There are two additional methods that you will eventually add to this menu. The first is an option for users to verify the data they entered. If the data is correct, which the users will tell the program after checking the data, then the data will be saved. If not, then the data will be removed from the variables and the users can input the data again. The second is an option to terminate the adding of records, or to continue and add more records.

You will add these methods to the program in later lessons. These methods are mentioned here because they are important when considering the design of the user interface. Your menus should have built-in safeguards to make users aware of their actions. Remember this when designing the layout of your other menus and screens.

Summary

This lesson focused on user interaction and how to empower the user to control certain aspects of a program. The first half of this lesson focused on menu design as a mechanism for user interaction with a program. You learned how to create a simple menu by adding labels and text fields, and limiting user choices to those listed on the menu.

You then went on to modify your menu by using buttons instead of labels. This type of menu is used much more frequently than the old text-type interfaces. One of the concerns you may have had is the fact that as your applet size changed the placement of your buttons changed. However, that was resolved with the use of the GridLayout layout manager.

The aesthetics of an interface—how logical and neat the interface looks—were discussed. This aspect of programming also touches on the user-friendliness of a program. Can the user operate the program without breaking into a sweat? Is it intuitive? Is it logical? Or, is the user continually frustrated at the way the program operates?

You then explored the data input interface. Before a program can do anything, it must have data to process. That's where these types of interfaces come into play. They assist the program in getting data from the user.

You have also touched slightly on objects and object-oriented programming. The components you create throughout this project book can be used over and over again.

LESSON 2 REVIEW QUESTIONS

SHORT ANSWER

Define the following in the space provided.

1. User interaction

_____

2. End user

_____

3. User-friendly

_____

4. Control

_____

_____

_____

5. GUI

_____

_____

6. Intuitive

_____

_____

7. Aesthetics

_____

8. Text fields

_____

_____

9. Buttons

_____

_____

10. Check box

_____

11. Objects

_____

_____

12. Object-oriented programming

_____

13. Choice control

_____

14. Inherit

_____

_____

15. Interface

_____

16. add ( )

_____

17. GridLayout

_____

18. Layout manager

_____

19. setText()

_____

WRITTEN QUESTIONS

Write your answers to the following questions in the space provided.

1. Why is it important that a program is user-friendly?

_____

_____

2. Explain the purpose of a user interface.

_____

_____

3. Explain how a user interface can provide the user with control over a program.

_____

_____

4. Explain aesthetics in terms of computer programming.

_____

_____

5. List the various components that may prove useful in constructing a user interface.

_____

_____

_____

_____

_____

_____

_____

6. Explain the following line of code (pulled from Project 2-4):

```
result.setText("You entered " + fname.getText() + " " + lname.getText() +
" " + email.getText() + ".");
```

_____

_____

_____

7. List and explain at least three types of "checks" that you should build into a user interface.

_____

_____

_____

_____

_____

_____

TESTING YOUR SKILLS

Estimated Time:

Application 2-1 45 minutes
Application 2-2 45 minutes
Application 2-3 1 ½ hours
Application 2-4 1 hour
Application 2-5 1 ½ hours

When you begin work on the Applications below, make sure you take time to scan through other software packages to see how they handle these menu choices.

APPLICATION 2-1

In Project 2-1 you built a text-based menu to allow the user to perform various tasks on a file. Add a heading to your simple text menu that reads "Records Menu."

1. Open the **Proj2_1.java** program file.

2. Rename both the class and the file as **App2_1.java**.

3. Add the heading **RECORDS MENU** to the menu.

4. Save your file.

5. Compile and run your applet.

APPLICATION 2-2

In Project 2-3 you built a component-based menu using buttons and the GridLayout layout manager to allow the user to perform various tasks on a file. Add a heading to your menu that reads "Records Menu" using components and the existing layout manager.

1. Open the **Proj2_3.java** program file.

2. Rename both the class and the file as **App2_2.java**.

3. Add the heading **RECORDS MENU** to the menu.

4. Save your file.

5. Compile and run your applet.

APPLICATION 2-3

In Project 2-1 you built a text-based menu to allow the user to perform various tasks on a file. Create an interface for the *MODIFY* menu item in Project 2-1. When you *modify* a record, you first need to display it to see if it is the correct record and then you need to modify the information that has changed. Design a simple "template" for the new interface.

1. Open a new program file.

2. Create and add the necessary components to your applet.

3. Prompt the user to input a last name to be used to search for the record to be modified.

4. Display a message that states that this is the record to be modifed upon the entering of the name.

5. Save your applet as **App2_3.java**.

6. Compile and run the program so that you can see the screen format.

APPLICATION 2-4

Create an interface screen for the *DELETE* menu item in Project 2-1. When you choose to *delete* a record you first need to make sure you are deleting the correct record. Use the code and screen design for App2_3 as a "template" for the interface.

1. Open the **App2_3.java** program file.

2. Print out the code to this program.

3. Compile and run the program so that you can see the screen format.

4. Change the code so that it displays a confimation message regarding the record to be deleted. (***HINT:*** Here we are trying to get rid of a specific record. Including a check line similar to "Is this the record you want to delete?" is a good idea.)

5. Save your file as **App2_4.java**.

6. Compile and run the program so that you can see the screen format.

APPLICATION 2-5

Create an interface screen for the *VIEW/PRINT* menu item in Project 2-1. This menu choice will most likely present another menu that provides a list of viewing or printing choices to be selected by the user. Use the code and screen design for Project 2-3 as a "template" for the interface.

1. Open the **Proj2_3.java** program file.

2. Print out the code to this program.

3. Compile and run the program so that you can see the screen format.

4. On scratch paper, manually design possible layouts for this Report menu. (***HINT:*** This menu item may lead to another more detailed menu. Does the user want to view or print? Can the print option be separate from the view option? Is there only one option, the "combined" VIEW/PRINT? You decide.)

5. Using Proj2_3 code as an example, code your screen layouts. Do *not* worry about the function of the menu—only code the layout.

6. Give each button you use a different report name, with the exception of the exit button.

7. Code a line of text to display as each report menu button is clicked.

8. Save your program as **App2_5.java**.

9. Compile and run your program so that you can see the screen format.

CRITICAL THINKING

Estimated Time: 4 hours

SCANS

In this lesson you focused on the creation of two types of user interfaces. One provided the user with choices to make in regard to program action. The second provided the user with an interface through which data could be entered in a record. In the Applications above, you were required to create interfaces from the other menu choices.

However, many other types of interfaces can make your program easier to use, as well as enabling the program to maintain control over its operation. For example, when you log on to your school's network you may be asked for a user name and password, or when you want to open a file you need to select a drive, folder, and so on, to create a path to that file.

Your Critical Thinking assignment is to create two additional user interfaces, not included in this lesson, using the two questions below as guidelines:

1. What *kind* of information will I be keeping track of?

2. What do I want to *do* with the information?

Once you have answered these questions, you can begin designing your user interfaces. Good luck and have fun!

CALCULATIONS

OBJECTIVES

On completion of this lesson, you should be able to:

■ Explain the purpose of calculations.

■ Explain the advantages and disadvantages of performing calculations versus storing values.

■ Demonstrate the appropriate use of calculations versus storing values.

■ Demonstrate the proper use of variables in calculations.

■ Explain the difference between primitive and nonprimitive data types.

■ Code the interaction between primitive and nonprimitive data types.

■ Relate your calculations to user interaction.

■ Translate math formulas into code.

■ Design code for including calculations in programs.

■ Distinguish precedence among the order of operators.

■ Place multiple applets on a Web page.

🕐 **Estimated Time: 5 ½ hours**

Introduction

Calculations are an important part of any computer program. Computers are always calculating something. It may be interest on a past due invoice; it may be payroll; it may be sports statistics; or it may be subtracting money from your checking account every time you use your ATM. Historically, and even today, computers have been used as "supercalculators."

The main purpose of a calculation is to find an answer. The end user needs to know something, so he or she "asks" the computer to perform the calculation. Why? Because the computer does it faster, and if it's programmed right, it won't make a mistake. Just like with user interfaces, calculations help make life easier for the end user.

41

This lesson will focus on the following:

■ **Learning the purpose of calculations.** The purpose behind including calculations in code will be continuously explained. It's not enough to know how; you also need to know why.

■ **Understanding the advantages and disadvantages of performing calculations versus storing values, and the appropriate use of calculations versus storing values.** When you develop code for a program, you will notice there are instances where the calculation is performed and the answer is output, but the answer is never stored. Some calculations are so simple and quick that it makes more sense to perform them when the answers are needed than to store the answers again and again in a file. For example, if you know that an employee worked 36 regular hours and 0 overtime hours, then you know the total hours, or you can calculate it quickly.

■ **Exploring the proper use of variables in calculations and how to relate calculations to user interaction.** As mentioned, you will be performing calculations needed by the end user. Therefore, you will need to gather information from the end user in order to perform the calculation so that it benefits that particular end user. The only way to get input from the end user is to use variables through a user interface, and these variables need to be defined and used properly.

■ **Learning the difference between primitive and nonprimitive data types and coding the interaction between primitive and nonprimitive data types.** The only nonobject data types in Java are the typical data types you may have been exposed to in other languages. These data types are as follows: BOOLEAN, CHAR, BYTE, SHORT INT, LONG, FLOAT, and DOUBLE. However, Java does have nonprimitive versions of these that are actually objects. You will interact with these two groups of data types in the applets in this lesson. One benefit of these primitive data types is that they *will* work across all computer platforms that support Java, unlike the C\C++ data types, which differ between platforms.

■ **Translating math formulas into code, designing code for including calculations in programs, distinguishing precedence among the order of operators, and analyzing your programs to determine their correctness.** These four objectives basically translate into programming. You will decide what calculations you need to perform, then you will find the appropriate math formula. At that point, you will begin to translate the formula into code. You will need to pay particular attention to precedence in order to make sure complex formulas are performed correctly. Finally, you will review the answer to make sure the calculation was performed correctly.

■ **Placing multiple applets on a Web page.** In place of running multiple windows inside an applet, which is difficult to do, you will place multiple applets within a single Web page.

■ **Producing working applications from the instructions provided.** You will code working applications in every lesson in this book. There is no better way to learn how to program than to program.

So, remember your math, get ready to work, and prepare to have fun!

P R O J E C T   3 - 1 :
Decimal to Hexadecimal, Octal, and Binary Conversion   Ⓑ

Once again you will start with simple programs and work your way into harder projects. In this lesson you will be required to do some research and coding on your own—nothing too hard, just enough to introduce you to what programmers *really* go through in coding their programs.

This project will perform decimal integer to hexadecimal, octal, and binary conversion. **String conversion methods** will perform the conversion calculation itself. Even though this is a shortcut, don't feel slighted because many items are built into Java that will make your programming jobs easier for you. These **objects** can be reused in many different programs, many different times. You will be doing the same with the calculations you create in these projects.

Step 1: Start Your Compiler

The projects in this book have been developed using the Microsoft Visual J++ 6.0 compiler. However, the programs you will be writing will work regardless of the version of Java used, or even if you use a simple text editor.

Step 2: Type in Your Code

Your code should be typed in exactly as follows. Save this program with the name **Proj3-1.java**. Remember to save your code after typing in the first line or two of your program, and then as often as possible thereafter.

```java
// Proj3_1

import java.awt.*;
import java.applet.*;
import java.awt.event.*;

public class Proj3_1 extends Applet implements ActionListener
{
    Label prompt1;
    TextField input1;
    int number;
    String hexstring, octstring, binstring;

    public void init()
    {
        prompt1 = new Label("Enter an integer then press enter: ");
        add(prompt1);

        input1 = new TextField(10);
        input1.addActionListener(this);
        add(input1);

    }

    public void actionPerformed(ActionEvent e)
    {
        number = Integer.parseInt(input1.getText());
        hexstring = Integer.toHexString(number).toUpperCase();
        octstring = Integer.toOctalString(number);
        binstring = Integer.toBinaryString(number);
        repaint();
    }

    public void paint (Graphics g)
```

```
    {
        g.drawString("The hexadecimal equivalent of the number you entered
is: " + hexstring, 20, 100);
        g.drawString("The octal equivalent of the number you entered is: "
+ octstring, 20, 120);
        g.drawString("The binary equivalent of the number you entered is:
" + binstring, 20, 140);
    }
}
```

Step 3: Save Your Program

Once you have finished typing in your code, save your code one final time before compiling your program.

Step 4: Compile and Run

Enter the commands necessary to compile and run your program. If you are running Visual J++ 6.0, simply click the **Run** button. Your applet will begin to compile. If there are no errors, your applet should run within the Microsoft Applet Viewer. If errors occur during the compile process, check your code, correct any errors, and rerun the program.

If you are not using Visual J++ 6.0 as your compiler, use the appropriate commands for your compiler. You should now be familiar with those commands.

Step 5: Review Your Code

Now that your program has run successfully, answer the following questions about the new code introduced in this project. Review the introductory comments preceding this project for additional help.

1. Explain the `import` command lines.

_____

_____

2. Explain the `Integer.toHexString()`.

_____

3. Explain the `Integer.toOctalString()`.

_____

4. Explain the `Integer.toBinaryString()`.

_____

5. Explain why `number` is an integer variable type.

_____

4 4

Step 6: Add Comments to Your Code

Add the appropriate comments in the appropriate places in your code. When you are finished, save your program.

1. List your comments, explain where they were placed, and explain why.

_____

_____

_____

Step 7: Recompile and Run Your Program

Changes you make to your program, even the simple insertion of comments, can cause your program not to run properly. Any time you modify your code, you need to recompile it. If any errors occur during this step, review the comments you entered and correct any errors.

Congratulations! You now have a very easy program that will convert decimal integers to hexadecimal, octal, and binary numbers.

PROJECT 3-2: Foreign Currency Conversions Ⓑ

If you haven't noticed, the world is becoming smaller. With the Internet we have instant access to anyone in the world who's connected. Getting information from one country to another is becoming easier and easier.

In light of this, many businesses, both large and small, are developing a global customer base. One of the concerns in the financial world is the conversion of foreign currency into dollars and vice versa. What makes this conversion especially difficult is that the values of most currencies are not fixed—they float (or fluctuate). Because of this, businesses need to keep track of currency values daily. You are going to code two programs that will help them do just that. The first project will convert foreign currency into dollars; the second will reverse the conversion.

You are also going to be expected to start remembering how to code the appropriate input for your programs. With this project, you will be asked to do more of the work. After all, it's what programmers are paid big bucks to do!

Step 1: Code the General Outline of the Main()

If you review all the programs you've coded, you will notice that the applets have a general layout. Write it down here.

_____

_____

_____

_____

_____

_____

Step 2: Start Your Compiler

If you need to, review previous projects in order to complete this step.

Step 3: Type in Your Code

Type in your code exactly as shown below. Save this program with the name **Proj3_2.java**. As you enter the code, add comments in the appropriate places.

```
// Proj3_2

import java.awt.*;
import java.applet.*;
import java.awt.event.*;

public class Proj3_2 extends Applet implements ActionListener
{
    Float forgnCurr, xRate;
    float dollars;
    Label forgnAmt, forgnName, forgnRate;
    TextField txtFC, txtName, txtRate;

    public void init()
    {
        forgnAmt = new Label("Enter the amount of foreign currency you
        have: ");
        add(forgnAmt);

        txtFC = new TextField(10);
        add(txtFC);

        forgnName = new Label("Enter the name of the foreign currency: ");
        add(forgnName);

        txtName = new TextField(10);
        add(txtName);

        forgnRate = new Label("Enter today's exchange rate for this
        currency: ");
        add(forgnRate);

        txtRate = new TextField(10);
        txtRate.addActionListener(this);
        add(txtRate);
    }

    public void actionPerformed(ActionEvent e)
    {
        forgnCurr = Float.valueOf(txtFC.getText());
        txtName.getText();
        xRate = Float.valueOf(txtRate.getText());
        dollars = forgnCurr.floatValue() * xRate.floatValue();
        repaint();
    }
```

```
public void paint (Graphics g)
{
        g.drawString("This amount of " + txtName.getText() + " converts to
" + dollars + " dollars.", 20, 150);
    }
}
```

Remember to save your code after typing in the first line or two of your program, and then as often as possible thereafter.

1. List your comments, where they were placed, and explain why.

_____

_____

_____

2. Explain why the Float variable type was used for the numeric variables.

_____

_____

3. Explain the difference between a nonprimitive Float and a primitive Float data type.

_____

_____

4. Explain the `Float.valueOf()`.

_____

_____

Step 4: Save Your Program

Once you have finished typing in the code, save it one final time before compiling your program.

Step 5: Compile Your Program

Enter the commands necessary to compile your program. If your program compiles properly, then *stop.* If errors occur during compile, check your code, correct any errors, and recompile the program.

At this point you should have a working program. Now we need some "real" data in order to run the program.

Step 6: Finding Data

Input the following foreign exchange rates. (***NOTE:*** These are only sample rates. You should be able to find actual, current rates in your local paper, on the Internet, or by calling your local bank.)

CURRENCY	FOREIGN CURRENCY IN $	$ IN FOREIGN CURRENCY
Dollar (Canada)	.6562	1.5239
Yen (Japan)	.008671	115.33
Peso (Mexico)	.100503	9.9500
Mark (Germany)	.6024	1.6601

Step 7: Run Your Program

Now that you have your data ready, run the program on your compiler. When prompted, input the requested information. The program will ask for the amount from the appropriate column.

Just to be sure the program is working properly, check the output with a calculator. If everything checks out, which it should, you have another working program!

PROJECT 3-3:
Dollar-to-Foreign Currency Conversions

Now, let's see what you've learned. You are going to code this project by yourself. All the information you need has already been presented to you. Follow the steps below and the hints provided to complete this project. Also, make sure you make use of the space provided to list the things you do inside each step.

This project is simple. Instead of converting foreign currency to dollars, you will be converting dollars into a foreign currency. Just think how useful this would be on your next business trip or vacation to some foreign locale!

Step 1: Code the General Outline of the Applet

In the space provided, outline the code needed for your applet class.

_____

_____

_____

_____

_____

_____

Step 2: Start Your Compiler

If your compiler is not running already, start it now.

Step 3: Type in Your Code

You need to write your code before you can type it in. Up to this point you've been given the code to key in. This time, you write the code. In Step 1 you outlined the applet class. Now, design the body of the code. Feel free to look back at previous examples, especially Proj3_2.

The first thing you should do is lay out the calculation needed for the program. You can do this with a diagram, *flowchart*, or *pseudocode*. Review the last project while observing what the program actually does. Print out the code and take a look at how the program functions as you run it. Your job is to code a program that does the conversion in the opposite direction. Give it some thought.

1. In the space below, lay out the calculation needed for this project.

_____

_____

_____

_____

_____

_____

_____

_____

_____

_____

_____

_____

_____

_____

_____

_____

_____

_____

_____

_____

_____

_____

Second, you need to identify your variables. You will notice from the code in Project 3-2 that the only variables needed were the ones used in the calculation. These variables were used for input, manipulation, and output. **REMEMBER:** Variable names and type should make sense in regard to the values they will contain and the calculation they will perform. The major difference here will be that the variables need to be named differently. In this case, the type can remain the same.

2. In the space below, list and name the variables you will use in this program. Explain the data types assigned to each variable.

_____

_____

_____

_____

_____

Third, set up your user interface and output lines. Remember that your program is working in reverse, so the sentences used in your prompts and outputs need to reflect that difference.

4 9

3. Edit the code for your user interface and output.

_____

_____

_____

_____

_____

_____

_____

_____

_____

_____

_____

_____

_____

_____

_____

_____

4. In the space below, organize your code. This way you can input it in the proper order.

_____

_____

_____

_____

_____

_____

_____

_____

_____

_____

_____

_____

_____

_____

_____

_____

_____

_____

_____

_____

_____

_____

_____

_____

_____

_____

5. Type in the code you have developed. Save the file as **Proj3_3.java**. Save your code repeatedly after every three or four lines.

Step 4: Save Your Program

Once you have finished typing in your code, save it one final time before compiling your program.

Step 5: Compile

Enter the commands necessary to compile your program. If your program compiles properly, then *stop*. If errors occur during the compile, check your code, correct any errors, and recompile the program.

Step 6: Finding Data

Use the same data listed in Step 6 of Project 3-2. Again, you can find current data in your local paper, by calling your local bank, or by searching the Internet.

Step 7: Run Your Program

Now that you have your data ready, run the program on your compiler. When prompted, input the requested information.

Just to be sure the program is working properly, check the output with a calculator. If everything checks out, which it should, you have another working program!

PROJECT 3-4:
Height Conversion—Feet and Inches to Centimeters and Meters

In this program, the calculations will be slightly harder. You will convert your height from feet and inches to meters and centimeters. Instead of writing two separate programs as you did earlier, you will include both calculations in the same applet.

Very rarely will you write a program that will perform one calculation and then terminate. You may write an *applet* that will perform a single calculation, maybe even multiple calculations, or multiple single-calculation applets that will be used on one Web page. This topic will be expanded on later in this lesson. Start with your multiple-calculation program.

Step 1: Start Your Compiler

If your compiler is not already running, start it now.

Step 2: Type in Your Code

Type in the code as shown below. Save the program as **Proj3_4.java**. *REMEMBER:* Save often as you type in the code. Add comments to your code as you enter it.

```
// Proj3_4

import java.awt.*;
import java.applet.*;
import java.awt.event.*;

public class Proj3_4 extends Applet implements ActionListener
{
    Double feet, inches;
    double tempInches, tempTotal, centMtr, mtr;
    Label lblFeet, lblInches;
    TextField txtFeet, txtInches;

    public void init()
    {
        lblFeet = new Label("Enter your height in feet ");
        add(lblFeet);

        txtFeet = new TextField(10);
        add(txtFeet);

        lblInches = new Label("and inches, then press Enter. ");
        add(lblInches);

        txtInches = new TextField(10);
        txtInches.addActionListener(this);
        add(txtInches);
    }

    public void actionPerformed(ActionEvent e)
    {
        feet = Double.valueOf(txtFeet.getText());
        inches = Double.valueOf(txtInches.getText());
        tempInches = feet.doubleValue() * 12;
        tempTotal = tempInches + inches.doubleValue();
        centMtr = tempTotal * 2.54;
        mtr = centMtr /100;
```

```
            repaint();
    }

    public void paint (Graphics g)
    {
            g.drawString("You are " + centMtr + " centimeters tall.", 20,
100);
            g.drawString("That converts to " + mtr + " meters tall.", 20,
120);
    }
}
```

1. List your comments, where they were placed, and explain why.

_____

_____

_____

_____

_____

_____

Step 3: Save Your Program

When you have finished typing the code, save your program once more before moving on to the next step.

Step 4: Compile and Run

Enter the commands necessary to compile and run your program. If errors occur, check your code, correct any errors, and rerun the program.

Remember to save your program any time you make changes!

When you run your program you will be prompted to enter your height, first in feet and then in inches. When you press Enter after entering the inches, your height will be calculated in both centimeters and meters.

You now have a program that performs a metric conversion. Additional metric conversion programs will now prove easy to create because all you have to do is rename variables and replace the calculation.

Step 5: Explain Your Program

Make sure you keep practicing your ability to analyze and explain Java code. Explain each line or block of code in the space provided.

```
import java.awt.*;
import java.applet.*;
import java.awt.event.*;
```

_____

_____

```
public class Proj3_4 extends Applet implements ActionListener
{
```

```
Double feet, inches;
double tempInches, tempTotal, centMtr, mtr;
Label lblFeet, lblInches;
TextField txtFeet, txtInches;
```

```
public void init()
{
        lblFeet = new Label("Enter your height in feet ");
        add(lblFeet);

        txtFeet = new TextField(10);
        add(txtFeet);

        lblInches = new Label("and inches, then press Enter. ");
        add(lblInches);

        txtInches = new TextField(10);
        txtInches.addActionListener(this);
        add(txtInches);
}
```

```
public void actionPerformed(ActionEvent e)
{
        feet = Double.valueOf(txtFeet.getText());
        inches = Double.valueOf(txtInches.getText());
        tempInches = feet.doubleValue() * 12;
        tempTotal = tempInches + inches.doubleValue();
        centMtr = tempTotal * 2.54;
        mtr = centMtr /100;
        repaint();
}
```

_____

_____

_____

_____

_____

_____

_____

_____

```
public void paint (Graphics g)
{
        g.drawString("You are " + centMtr + " centimeters tall.", 20,
        100);
        g.drawString("That converts to " + mtr + " meters tall.", 20,
        120);
}
```

_____

_____

_____

_____

_____

_____

When you're finished, compare your answers with those of your teacher and classmates to reinforce your ability to analyze Java code.

The last calculation you will code deals with borrowing short-term money from the bank. Many businesses and individuals borrow various amounts of money for short time periods to meet financial obligations. They then pay this money back, usually in a number of months, with simple interest added on. Simple interest is interest calculated on the principal (the amount borrowed) only; there is no compounding (charging interest on interest) involved as with long-term borrowing.

In this project, we will discuss **precedence**. Precedence is the order in which **arithmetic operators** are applied within a formula. This order is the same as in algebra. Arithmetic operations are performed in the following order:

```
(   )
*, /, or %
+ or –
```

It's important to know in which order these operators are applied. If you do not pay attention to precedence, you will end up with an arithmetic calculation that does *not* do what you expect! Use parentheses to establish which operations are carried out first. Since the operators inside parentheses are applied first, simply use parentheses to segregate the portions of your multiple calculations. Parentheses also help make your code more readable. Anyone looking at code will find it easier to follow if your calculations, at least the harder ones, are segregated with parentheses.

Step 1: Start Your Compiler

If your compiler is not already running, start it now.

Step 2: Type in Your Code

Type in the code as shown below. Save the program as **Proj3_5.java**. *REMEMBER:* Save often as you type in the code. Add comments to your code as you enter it.

```java
// Proj3_5

import java.awt.*;
import java.applet.*;
import java.awt.event.*;

public class Proj3_5 extends Applet implements ActionListener
{
    Float principal, intRate, months;
    double period, payment;
    Label lblPrin, lblInterest, lblMonths;
    TextField txtPrin, txtInterest, txtMonths;

    public void init()
    {
        lblPrin = new Label("Enter the amount you will borrow: ");
        add(lblPrin);
```

```
        txtPrin = new TextField(10);
        add(txtPrin);

        lblInterest = new Label("Enter the interest % you will be charged:
");
        add(lblInterest);

        txtInterest = new TextField(10);
        add(txtInterest);

        lblMonths = new Label("Enter the # of months you will use the
money: ");
        add(lblMonths);

        txtMonths = new TextField(10);
        txtMonths.addActionListener(this);
        add(txtMonths);
    }

    public void actionPerformed(ActionEvent e)
    {
        principal = Float.valueOf(txtPrin.getText());
        intRate = Float.valueOf(txtInterest.getText());
        months = Float.valueOf(txtMonths.getText());

        period = months.floatValue() * 30/365;
        payment = principal.floatValue() + (principal.floatValue()
*((intRate.floatValue() / 100) * period));
        repaint();
    }

    public void paint (Graphics g)
    {
        g.drawString("The total amount you will owe in " +
months.floatValue() + " months will be " + payment, 20, 150);

    }
}
```

1. List your comments, where they were placed, and explain why.

_____

_____

_____

_____

_____

_____

Step 3: Save Your Program

When you have finished typing the code, save your program once more before moving on to the next step.

Step 4: Compile and Run

Enter the commands necessary to compile and run your program. If errors occur during either of these processes, check your code, correct any errors, and rerun the program.

Remember to save your program any time you make changes!

When you run your program, you will be prompted to enter the amount you want to borrow (principal), the interest rate you will be charged (for example, 9.75), and the number of months for which you would like to borrow the money. When you press Enter, you will be shown the amount of money you will need to pay back to the bank.

Step 5: Explain Your Program

Make sure you keep practicing your ability to analyze and explain Java code. Let's focus on the line of code shown below containing the calculation:

```
period = months.floatValue() * 30/365;
```

Interest rates are technically an annual percentage rate (APR). Because the interest percent you entered is the interest for an entire year, you need to proportion the part of the year for which you borrowed the money. So, in this line of code the number of months you entered is multiplied by 30 and then divided by 365.

If you remember operator precedence, you will know that the * and / operators are at the same level of precedence; therefore, those operations are performed first, beginning at the left.

1. Rewrite this line of code in the space below, using parentheses to make the code easier to read.

_____

Now take a look at the next line:

```
payment = principal.floatValue() + (principal.floatValue()
*((intRate.floatValue() / 100) * period));
```

This line of code makes liberal use of parentheses. It may look complicated at first; however, if you break it down one set of parentheses at a time, you will see how easy it is to read.

Start with the innermost set of parentheses: `(intRate.floatValue()/100)`. This portion of the calculation takes the interest rate that you entered and divides it by 100. This converts the interest rate, as you like to see it (for example, 9.75), into the decimal equivalent needed by the calculation (.0975).

The next set of parentheses—`((intRate.floatValue()/100)*period))`—takes the answer from the first part and multiplies it by the answer from the first line of code you reviewed. If you had actually entered 9.75 as your interest percent, this line of code would appear as `((.0975) * period)`.

Next, move to the last set of parentheses: `(principal.floatValue() * ((intRate.floatValue()/100) * period))`. Here, you are simply multiplying the principal (the amount of money you borrowed) by the answer from your first two sets of parentheses.

Walk through these two lines, step by step using actual numbers.

If, when asked for the number of months, you had entered the number 3, the first line of code would have calculated the following:

$3 * 30 = 90$, then $90 / 365 = .2465753$ (or an approximate number).

Then the program would have moved on to the next line of code. The first calculation to be performed on the next line would be (intRate/100). Using the interest rate from the review above, this calculation would perform the following:

$9.75 / 100 = .0975$

The calculation in the second set of parentheses would perform as follows:

$.0975 * .2465753$ (from the previous line of code) $= .0240411$

The calculation in your last set of parentheses would then multiply your principal by the answer above. If you had borrowed $1,000.00, the calculation would be performed as follows:

$1000 * .0240411 = 24.041096$

The two lines of code up to this point have calculated the amount of simple interest you will have to pay back to the bank *in addition* to the amount you borrowed. This leads us to the last calculation on this line: principal.floatValue() + (principal.floatValue() * ((intRate.floatValue() / 100) * period)).

All you have left to do is to add the amount of interest that you calculated to the amount of money that you borrowed. This last part of the calculation will be performed as follows:

$1000 + 24.041096 = 1024.041096$

Therefore, if you borrow $1,000.00 from the bank for three months at 9.75%, you will need to repay the bank $1,024.04 three months from the day you borrow the money. As you can see, this program will prove useful to anyone borrowing money for a short period of time.

PROJECT 3-6 : Multiple Applets

This project will take the Java program files from each of the first three projects and combine them on one Web page. This project will be based on Microsoft's Visual J++ 6.0. Your instructor will be able to provide you with the necessary replacement steps to make this work with your Java compiler if you are not using Visual J++.

Step 1: Start Your Compiler

If your compiler is not already running, start it now.

Step 2: Open a New Project

When a new project is open in Visual J++ it includes a Web page and a Java file by default. The Web page is named Page1.htm and the Java file is named Applet1.java. Save this project as **Proj3_6**. The compiler will add its own Microsoft J++ extension to the project. Remember to save your project *after every step*.

Step 3: Remove Applet1.java from the Project

Highlight the **Applet1.java** file without opening it. Click **Project** on the menu bar, then select the **Remove From Project** option. This will remove the highlighted item from your project.

Step 4: Add the Applets to the Project

Add the applets you want included. Click **Project** on the menu bar and select the **Add Item** option. A dialog box will open that has two tabs—New and Existing. Click on the **Existing** tab. Open the folder containing the files for the first three projects in this lesson, and double-click the Java file icons for these projects. They will appear in the Project Explorer window.

Step 5: Add the Applets to the Web Page

Double-click the **Page1.htm** icon in the Project Explorer. The code window will transform into a tabbed window. Click the **Source** tab. This view of the Web page will provide you with the source code. However, the default is to show controls (applets) graphically. Click **View** on the menu bar, then select **View Controls As Text** from the menu. This will convert the graphics to text. The following block of code will be shown:

```
<APPLET class="" code=Applet1.class height=200 name=Applet1
    style="LEFT: 0px; TOP: 0px" width=350>
<PARAM NAME="foreground" VALUE="FFFFFF">
<PARAM NAME="background" VALUE="008080">
<PARAM NAME="label" VALUE="This string was passed from the HTML
    host."></APPLET>
```

Copy and paste this block of code two times inside the Page1.htm Web page. Then change the *code=Applet1.class* property to **Proj3_1.class** in the original block, to **Proj3_2** in the second block, and to **Proj3_3** in the third block. You will also need to change the *name=Applet1* property in the second and third applet blocks to **Applet2** and **Applet3**. This will make sure each applet control that's contained on the Web page has a unique name.

Step 6: Make Sure Page1.htm Starts by Default

Click **Project** on the menu bar, then select the **Proj3_6 Properties** option. A dialog box with the Launch tab displayed opens. The first option button is *Default*. Directly underneath that choice a heading appears that reads *When project runs, load . . .*. Under that heading is a drop-down list box that should contain the name of your Web page, Page1.htm. If it does not contain the Page1.htm name, click on the list box arrow and select that file as the default, then click **OK**. If it does contain that filename, click **OK**.

Step 7: Save Your Project

When you have finished changing the code, save your project once more before moving on to the next step.

Step 8: Run

Enter the commands necessary to run your project. You should not experience any compile errors since the applets have been corrected previously. However, if you do encounter errors, correct them, and rerun the project.

Remember to save your project any time you make changes!

These applets should ask for the same information as they did originally. The difference will be that they will each be running independently of each other within the same Web page.

Your Web page will open in your browser. Maximize the browser window in order to see the first two projects side by side and the third project directly below the first as shown in Figure 3-1.

FIGURE 3-1
Multiple applets within Web page

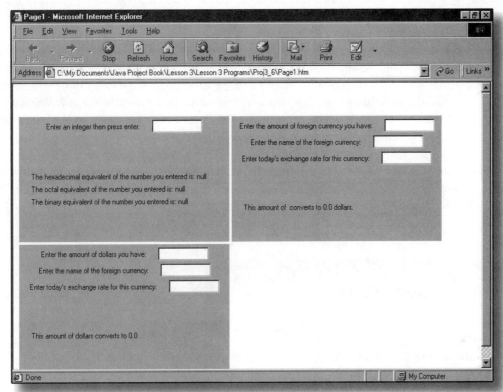

Performing Calculations vs. Storing Values

Should you perform calculations every time you need an answer, or should you save the answer for later use? This is an important issue when performing calculations.

The best way to answer this question overall is to compare processing time to storage space. The question is: Will it be easier on your system to perform the calculation once, and then store the answer? Or will it be easier to perform the calculation every time without storing the answer at all? The answer depends on the system and how the system administrator is trying to optimize the system's performance.

Your job is to make sure your programs help optimize the system or at least run within the established framework. And the best way to do this is to discuss things with your system administrator. In the world of ***distributed processing***—computing that takes place on multiple machines in multiple locations—you as a programmer need to be aware of system ***infrastructures*** and system ***capabilities***. Start now in learning about systems by discussing things with your school's system administrator or technology coordinator.

Summary

Y̶ou focused on calculations in this lesson. You began with a simple calculation that was basically an output manipulator. Then you moved on to programs that required you to code the actual calculations or conversions. The one important feature of every program is the requirement of collecting data from the user. As a programmer, you will not know the needs of every user; therefore, you need to write your programs so that each user can get the desired solution.

Variables were also stressed: meaningful variable names, necessary variable types, and the use of variables within the program that the user never sees. These are all important aspects of making your program readable.

When you moved into complex calculations, precedence was discussed. It's crucial that your calculations work correctly. If you are not aware of the order in which operations are carried out, it is likely that your calculations will not work correctly. Use parentheses to control the order of operations.

You also learned the difference between Java's nonprimitive data types, which are objects, and the primitive data types which are the types you may be familiar with from exposure to other languages. You coded interactions between the two in order to become familiar with the nonprimitive versions.

And last but not least, you moved your applets into a Web page. By doing simple modifications of the Web page code you were able to add two additional applets to the same page. Since applets are usually meant to perform a single purpose, the simplest way to execute multiple applets is to add them to a single Web page. After all, this is where applets basically live!

LESSON 3 REVIEW QUESTIONS

SHORT ANSWER

Define the following in the space provided.

1. .toHexString()

   _____

   _____

2. .toOctalString()

   _____

3. .toBinaryString()

   _____

4. Primitive data types

   _____

5. Nonprimitive data types

   _____

6. Flowchart

_____

7. Pseudocode

_____

_____

8. Precedence

_____

_____

9. Parentheses

_____

10. Import

_____

11. HTML

_____

12. Arithmetic operators

_____

13. BOOLEAN, CHAR, BYTE, SHORT, INT, LONG, FLOAT, DOUBLE

_____

_____

14. `Float.valueOf()`

_____

15. `.floatValue()`

_____

16. `Double.valueOf()`

_____

17. `doubleValue()`

_____

18. code= property from Web page

_____

WRITTEN QUESTIONS

Write your answers to the following questions in the space provided.

1. What is the main purpose of a calculation?

   _____

2. Why is it important for calculations to perform correctly?

   _____

   _____

3. How can flowcharting or pseudocoding be helpful in designing your code?

   _____

   _____

   _____

   _____

4. Explain the importance of meaningful variable names.

   _____

   _____

5. Explain the importance of assigning the correct data type to a variable.

   _____

   _____

   _____

6. Explain the difference between primitive and nonprimitive data types.

   _____

   _____

   _____

   _____

7. Explain the advantage of primitive data types in Java.

   _____

   _____

   _____

8. List all the arithmetic operators in their order of precedence.

   _____

   _____

   _____

9. Explain how to add multiple applets to a single Web page.

_____

_____

_____

_____

_____

_____

_____

_____

_____

10. What is the "trade-off" when deciding to store data or to simply rerun a calculation every time you need an answer?

_____

_____

_____

TESTING YOUR SKILLS

Estimated Time:
Application 3-1 2 hours
Application 3-2 1 hour

APPLICATION 3-1

In Project 3-5, you created a program that would calculate simple interest on a short-term loan. One alternative that banks give to customers who borrow short-term is to *discount* their loan. This means that the customer allows the bank to subtract the amount of interest from the loan proceeds (the amount of money the customer receives). Then, when customers repay the loan, they only have to repay the amount borrowed. For example, if you were to borrow $1,000 for 12 months at 10% interest, then you would owe the bank $1,100 when you repaid the loan. The interest would be $100. Discounting would allow you to pay the $100 interest upfront. If you chose to do that, you would only receive $900 from the bank ($1,000 – $100 interest). However, at the end of the 12 months you would only repay the $1,000, since you had already paid the interest.

1. Open the **Proj3_5.java** program file.

2. Print out the code to this program.

3. Redesign the calculation so that the interest is subtracted.

4. Change the output line so that it informs the borrower how much their proceeds are.

5. Save the modified code as **App3_1.java**.

6. Compile and run your applet. If there are any errors, correct them, and then recompile the applet.

APPLICATION 3-2

Add the App3_1.java file to your Project 3-6 Web page.

1. Open the **Proj3_6** project file.

2. Add the **App3_1.java** file to this project as shown in Project 3-6.

3. Modify the Web page code to this project so that it includes **App3_1.class** when it opens.

4. Save the modified project as **App3_2**. The compiler will add its own Microsoft J++ project extension.

5. Run the project. If there are any errors, correct them, and then rerun it.

CRITICAL THINKING

Estimated Time: 6–8 hours

Create a list of calculations that will prove useful to you. In this lesson you used short-term loan calculations, foreign currency translations, metric conversions, and numbering system conversions. Each profession has calculations that are useful on a daily basis.

Select a group of useful calculations and write code for these calculations. For example, create an applet for baseball statistics (batting average, earned run average, slugging percentage, fielding percentage) or other sports statistics, grade calculations, exercise/workout records, or anything else of interest to you.

When you are finished writing the code and saving your applets, modify a single Web page so that it runs a handful of your applets simultaneously.

DECISION MAKING

Copying/scanning is not permitted and may be a violation of copyright laws.
© 2001 by South-Western Educational Publishing.

OBJECTIVES

On completion of this lesson, you should be able to:

■ Explain control structures.

■ Demonstrate the use of sequence and selection control structures.

■ Discriminate between the use of the if, the if/else, and the switch selection structures.

■ Design code that utilizes the three selection structures.

■ Revise earlier projects by integrating selection structures.

■ Analyze your programs to determine their correctness.

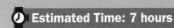 **Estimated Time: 7 hours**

Introduction

In developing a program, you must give users the opportunity to choose what they need to do with the program. Rarely, if at all, do you encounter a program that allows the user to do just *one* thing. If you think back to Lesson 2, you will remember that you designed screens that allowed the user to interact with your program. The menu screens provided the user with choices. Those user interfaces, however, lacked *functionality*. You will add that functionality in this lesson.

Control structures let you add this type of functionality to user interfaces and to other portions of a program. A control structure is a tool that directs the user to "jump" to other functions and procedures. There are seven types of control structures, which are grouped into three categories: *sequence*, *selection*, and *repetition*.

You're already familiar with sequence programming, in which your instructions are structured in a top-down manner and basically execute one right after another. Repetition will be addressed in Lesson 5. In this lesson, the selection category is addressed.

Think of selection as *decision making*. You are required to make a choice, or selection. Then based on your selection, the program does something. Another selection would cause the program to do something else. And that's almost all there is to it!

Decision making, or selection, uses three different structures: *if*, *if/else*, and *switch*. You have used the if structure in earlier lessons, specifically in Project 2-1. If you remember, you used five if statements to decide which choice the user was making from a simple menu. Based on the user's choice, something would happen. In these projects it was to add, modify, delete, view/print a record, or exit the program. You will use the if structure again by expanding your simple menu.

The if/else structure provides a simple "fork in the road" decision. If a condition is true you follow one road. If the condition is false, you take the other road. The switch structure is a multi-selection option. Instead of offering only two alternate "roads," the switch allows the user to select from many choices.

This lesson will focus on the following:

- **Understanding control structures and the use of sequence and selection control structures.** You will apply these two types of control structures.

- **Discriminating between the use of the *if*, the *if/else*, and the *switch* selection structures, and designing code that utilizes them.** You will learn the appropriate uses of the three selection structures, and you will be given the opportunity to design the code necessary to make them work.

- **Revising earlier projects by integrating selection structures.** As you progress from lesson to lesson, you are adding useful features to your programs. Now it's time to combine the features into cohesive functions, procedures, and programs. For example, you will be modifying your simple menu from Project 2-1 through the use of selection control structures.

- **Analyzing your programs to determine their correctness.** This part of programming never ends. The bottom line is that your programs must work properly. If you continue to develop your understanding of Java by constantly analyzing your programs, you will be the better for it in the long run because you will have developed good work habits.

So, get out your road maps, remember how to make decisions, and prepare to have fun!

P R O J E C T   4 - 1 : Simple Menu Review   Ⓑ

Start this project by reviewing your simple menu project from Lesson 2. In that project, you made use of the if structure.

Step 1: Start Your Compiler

Start your compiler if it is not already running. Open **Proj2_1.java** so that you can review the code.

Step 2: Print Your Code

Print the code from Proj2_1.java. You'll use this code because it is the "finished" version of your simple menu. It will be easier to complete this first project by having a hard copy of the code to which you can refer.

Your code should look like the following:

```
// Proj2_1.java
// Menu Choices


// The base classes from which your applet inherits
```

```java
import java.awt.*;
import java.applet.*;
import java.awt.event.*;

// Your class definition - it extends applet
// and will "listen" for an action
public class Proj2_1 extends Applet implements ActionListener
{

    // Your member variables
    Label choice1, choice2, choice3, choice4, choice5, prompt1;
    TextField selection;

    // Remember that an int is a primitive data type
    int number;

    // This method contains the things that happen when your applet
    // initializes
    public void init()
    {

        // You add 6 new labels and one new text field to your applet
        choice1 = new Label("1 - Enter A New Record.");
        add(choice1);

        choice2 = new Label("2 - Modify An Existing Record.");
        add(choice2);

        choice3 = new Label("3 - Delete An Existing Record.");
        add(choice3);

        choice4 = new Label("4 - View/Print An Existing Record.");
        add(choice4);

        choice5 = new Label("5 - Exit");
        add(choice5);

        prompt1 = new Label("   Enter Your Choice: ");
        add(prompt1);

        selection = new TextField(3);
        add(selection);
        selection.addActionListener(this);
    }

    // When data is entered into the text field and the enter key is pressed
    // the actions in this method are performed
    public void actionPerformed(ActionEvent e)
    {
        number = Integer.parseInt(selection.getText());
        repaint();
    }
```

```
// This paint method displays "text strings" on your applet
// depending on the choice the user makes
public void paint(Graphics g)
{
     if (number == 1)
          g.drawString("You chose to add a record.", 70, 150);
     if (number == 2)
          g.drawString("You chose to modify a record.", 70, 150);
     if (number == 3)
          g.drawString("You chose to delete a record.", 70, 150);
     if (number == 4)
          g.drawString("You chose to view/print a record.", 70, 150);
     if (number == 5)
          g.drawString("Close the browser window to stop execution!",
70, 150);
  }

}
```

If your code does not look like this, make the necessary modifications, and then save the program. After saving the program, compile and run it, correcting any errors necessary in order for it to run properly. Save the program one final time. Then print a hard copy.

Step 3: Review Your Code

Concentrate on reviewing the lines of code shown below.

```
     if (number == 1)
          g.drawString("You chose to add a record.", 70, 150);
     if (number == 2)
          g.drawString("You chose to modify a record.", 70, 150);
     if (number == 3)
          g.drawString("You chose to delete a record.", 70, 150);
     if (number == 4)
          g.drawString("You chose to view/print a record.", 70, 150);
     if (number == 5)
          g.drawString("Close the browser window to stop execution!",
70, 150);
```

This code is a good example of the if selection structure. Each line is structured the same, the only difference being that each choice will cause something different to happen.

1. Explain, in general, what happens when any of the five lines are executed.

_____

_____

2. Is using the if structure in this way comparable to using the if/else structure? Why or why not?

_____

_____

3. In the space below, add an if statement that will test for incorrect selections. Save your modified code as **Proj4_1.java**.

_____

_____

_____

_____

_____

_____

_____

_____

_____

_____

Step 4: Compile and Run

Enter the commands necessary to compile and run your program. If errors occur during the compile, check your code, correct any errors, and rerun the program.

Step 5: Test Your Program

Now that your program has run successfully, test the logic behind your code by entering various numbers and characters. If your program responds correctly, then the program is correct. If it doesn't, then you need to correct your code and recompile and rerun the program.

 HOT TIP

Java applets are always running once they start. They will execute condition tests even before a value is input.

Step 6: Review Your Code

Your code should look similar to the following:

```
// Proj4_1.java
// Menu Choices

// The base classes from which your applet inherits
import java.awt.*;
import java.applet.*;
import java.awt.event.*;

// Your class definition - it extends applet
// and will "listen" for an action
public class Proj4_1 extends Applet implements ActionListener
{

    // Your member variables
    Label choice1, choice2, choice3, choice4, choice5, prompt1;
    TextField selection;

    // Remember that an int is a primitive data type
    int number;
```

```java
// This method contains the things that happen when your applet
// initializes
public void init()
{

        // You add 6 new labels and one new text field to your applet
        choice1 = new Label("1 - Enter A New Record.");
        add(choice1);

        choice2 = new Label("2 - Modify An Existing Record.");
        add(choice2);

        choice3 = new Label("3 - Delete An Existing Record.");
        add(choice3);

        choice4 = new Label("4 - View/Print An Existing Record.");
        add(choice4);

        choice5 = new Label("5 - Exit");
        add(choice5);

        prompt1 = new Label("    Enter Your Choice: ");
        add(prompt1);

        selection = new TextField(3);
        add(selection);
        selection.addActionListener(this);
}

// When data is entered into the text field and the Enter key is pressed
// the actions in this method are performed
public void actionPerformed(ActionEvent e)
{
        number = Integer.parseInt(selection.getText());
        repaint();
}

// This paint method displays "text strings" on your applet
// depending on the choice the user makes.
// A straight if structure is used here.
public void paint(Graphics g)
{
        if (number == 1)
            g.drawString("You chose to add a record.", 70, 150);
        if (number == 2)
            g.drawString("You chose to modify a record.", 70, 150);
        if (number == 3)
            g.drawString("You chose to delete a record.", 70, 150);
        if (number == 4)
            g.drawString("You chose to view/print a record.", 70, 150);
        if (number == 5)
            g.drawString("Close the browser window to stop execution!",
```

```
70, 150);
          if (number != 1 && number != 2 && number !=3 && number != 4 &&
number != 5)
                g.drawString("Incorrect choice - please enter 1 - 5", 70,
170);
   }

}
```

1. You will notice that the final statement tests for an incorrect selection. Explain the execution of this statement.

_____

_____

_____

_____

You now have a working example of an if selection structure that also tests for incorrect selections. You should be able to use this type of structure in appropriate places in all of your programs!

PROJECT 4-2 : If/Else Structure

In this project you will convert the if structure used in Project 4-1 into an if/else structure. You will use this project to compare the differences between the two types of control structures.

Step 1: Start Your Compiler

Start your compiler if it is not already running. Open **Proj4_1.java** so that you can review the code.

Step 2: Print Your Code

Print the code from Proj4_1.java. The code should look like the following:

```
// Proj4_1.java
// Menu Choices

// The base classes from which your applet inherits
import java.awt.*;
import java.applet.*;
import java.awt.event.*;

// Your class definition - it extends applet
// and will "listen" for an action
public class Proj4_1 extends Applet implements ActionListener
{

    // Your member variables
    Label choice1, choice2, choice3, choice4, choice5, prompt1;
```

```
TextField selection;

// Remember that an int is a primitive data type
int number;

// This method contains the things that happen when your applet
// initializes
public void init()
{

        // You add 6 new labels and one new text field to your applet
        choice1 = new Label("1 - Enter A New Record.");
        add(choice1);

        choice2 = new Label("2 - Modify An Existing Record.");
        add(choice2);

        choice3 = new Label("3 - Delete An Existing Record.");
        add(choice3);

        choice4 = new Label("4 - View/Print An Existing Record.");
        add(choice4);

        choice5 = new Label("5 - Exit");
        add(choice5);

        prompt1 = new Label("    Enter Your Choice: ");
        add(prompt1);

        selection = new TextField(3);
        add(selection);
        selection.addActionListener(this);
}

// When data is entered into the text field and the Enter key is pressed
// the actions in this method are performed
public void actionPerformed(ActionEvent e)
{
        number = Integer.parseInt(selection.getText());
        repaint();
}

// This paint method displays "text strings" on your applet
// depending on the choice the user makes.
// A straight if structure is used here.
public void paint(Graphics g)
{
        if (number == 1)
              g.drawString("You chose to add a record.", 70, 150);
        if (number == 2)
              g.drawString("You chose to modify a record.", 70, 150);
        if (number == 3)
              g.drawString("You chose to delete a record.", 70, 150);
```

```
        if (number == 4)
            g.drawString("You chose to view/print a record.", 70, 150);
        if (number == 5)
            g.drawString("Close the browser window to stop execution!",
70, 150);
        if (number != 1 && number != 2 && number !=3 && number != 4 &&
number != 5)
            g.drawString("Incorrect choice - please enter 1 - 5", 70,
170);
    }

}
```

If your code does not look like this, make the necessary modifications and then save your program. After saving the program, compile and run it, correcting any errors necessary in order for it to run properly. Save the program one final time. Then print a hard copy.

Step 3: Convert the If Structure to an If/Else Structure

In the if structure, if any line is true, then the attached event happens. You can make this entire sequence execute faster by using **nested** if/else statements. Nested if/else statements make the code execute faster because as soon as one condition proves true, the sequence terminates.

1. In the space below, write the code for the if/else structure. This will be a nested if/else structure because you are testing for multiple occurrences. In the first five lines of code, the only changes will occur at the beginning of the line. In the last line, the one that tests for invalid selections, there will be a "major" modification. Save your modified code as **Proj4_2.java**.

_____

_____

_____

_____

_____

_____

_____

_____

_____

_____

_____

Step 4: Compile and Run

Enter the commands necessary to compile and run your program. If errors occur during the compile, check your code, correct any errors, and rerun the program.

Step 5: Test Your Program

Now that your program has run successfully, test the logic behind your code by entering various numbers and characters. If your program responds correctly, your program is correct. If it doesn't, you need to correct your code and recompile and rerun the program.

Step 6: Review Your Code

Your code should look similar to the following:

```java
// Proj4_2.java
// Menu Choices

// The base classes from which your applet inherits
import java.awt.*;
import java.applet.*;
import java.awt.event.*;

// Your class definition - it extends applet
// and will "listen" for an action
public class Proj4_2 extends Applet implements ActionListener
{

    // Your member variables
    Label choice1, choice2, choice3, choice4, choice5, prompt1;
    TextField selection;

    // Remember that an int is a primitive data type
    int number;

    // This method contains the things that happen when your applet
    // initializes
    public void init()
    {

        // You add 6 new labels and one new text field to your applet
        choice1 = new Label("1 - Enter A New Record.");
        add(choice1);

        choice2 = new Label("2 - Modify An Existing Record.");
        add(choice2);

        choice3 = new Label("3 - Delete An Existing Record.");
        add(choice3);

        choice4 = new Label("4 - View/Print An Existing Record.");
        add(choice4);

        choice5 = new Label("5 - Exit");
        add(choice5);

        prompt1 = new Label("    Enter Your Choice: ");
        add(prompt1);
```

```
            selection = new TextField(3);
            add(selection);
            selection.addActionListener(this);
    }

    // When data is entered into the text field and the Enter key is pressed
    // the actions in this method are performed
    public void actionPerformed(ActionEvent e)
    {
            number = Integer.parseInt(selection.getText());
            repaint();
    }

    // This paint method displays "text strings" on your applet
    // depending on the choice the user makes.
    // The if/else if structure is used here.
    public void paint(Graphics g)
    {
            if (number == 1)
                    g.drawString("You chose to add a record.", 70, 150);
            else if (number == 2)
                    g.drawString("You chose to modify a record.", 70, 150);
            else if (number == 3)
                    g.drawString("You chose to delete a record.", 70, 150);
            else if (number == 4)
                    g.drawString("You chose to view/print a record.", 70, 150);
            else if (number == 5)
                    g.drawString("Close the browser window to stop execution!",
70, 150);
            else g.drawString("Incorrect choice - please enter 1 - 5", 70,
170);
    }

}
```

1. You will notice that the final statement is simply an else statement. Explain why this is not an if/else statement.

_____

_____

2. Explain why you do not need to list all the valid choices as you did with the if structure.

_____

_____

You now have a working example of the if/else structure. You will be able to use this type of structure in the appropriate places in your programs!

In this project, you'll modify your simple menu one more time. This time you'll use a switch selection structure. Remember that the switch structure is used when you have multiple options from which to choose. Menus are ideal for the switch structure.

You'll take a look at the switch structure in two different ways. One will be within the current menu code, and the other will be by redefining your menu components.

Step 1: Start Your Compiler

Start your compiler if it is not already running.

Step 2: Modify Your Code

Open the **Proj4_1.java** file. Save it as **Proj4_3.java**. Modify the code exactly as shown below. Remember to save your code as you modify it.

```java
// Proj4_3.java
// Menu Choices

// The base classes from which your applet inherits
import java.awt.*;
import java.applet.*;
import java.awt.event.*;

// Your class definition - it extends applet
// and will "listen" for an action
public class Proj4_3 extends Applet implements ActionListener
{

    // Your member variables
    Label choice1, choice2, choice3, choice4, choice5, prompt1;
    TextField selection;

    // Remember that an int is a primitive data type
    int number;

    // This method contains the things that happen when your applet
    // initializes
    public void init()
    {

        // You add 6 new labels and one new text field to your applet
        choice1 = new Label("1 - Enter A New Record.");
        add(choice1);

        choice2 = new Label("2 - Modify An Existing Record.");
        add(choice2);

        choice3 = new Label("3 - Delete An Existing Record.");
        add(choice3);

        choice4 = new Label("4 - View/Print An Existing Record.");
```

```
            add(choice4);

            choice5 = new Label("5 - Exit");
            add(choice5);

            prompt1 = new Label("    Enter Your Choice: ");
            add(prompt1);

            selection = new TextField(3);
            add(selection);
            selection.addActionListener(this);
    }

    // When data is entered into the text field and the Enter key is pressed
    // the actions in this method are performed
    public void actionPerformed(ActionEvent e)
    {
            number = Integer.parseInt(selection.getText());
            repaint();
    }

    // This paint method displays "text strings" on your applet
    // depending on the choice the user makes.
    // The switch structure is used here.
    public void paint(Graphics g)
    {
            switch(number)
            {
            case 1:
                        g.drawString("You chose to add a record.", 70, 150);
                        break;
            case 2:
                        g.drawString("You chose to modify a record.", 70,
                        150);
                        break;
            case 3:
                        g.drawString("You chose to delete a record.", 70,
                        150);
                        break;
            case 4:
                        g.drawString("You chose to view/print a record.", 70,
                        150);
                        break;
            case 5:
                        g.drawString("Close the browser window to stop
                        execution!", 70, 150);
                        break;
            default:
                        g.drawString("Incorrect choice - please enter 1 - 5",
                        70, 170);
                        break;
            }
    }
}
```

Step 3: Compile and Run

Enter the commands necessary to compile and run your program. If errors occur during the compile, check your code, correct any errors, and recompile the program.

Test your program by selecting all the valid choices and by making a few invalid choices.

Step 4: Review Your Code

Let's take a look at the entire switch structure since it is very similar from line to line.

```
switch(number)
{
case 1:
        g.drawString("You chose to add a record.", 70, 150);
        break;
case 2:
        g.drawString("You chose to modify a record.", 70,
        150);
        break;
case 3:
        g.drawString("You chose to delete a record.", 70,
        150);
        break;
case 4:
        g.drawString("You chose to view/print a record.", 70,
        150);
        break;
case 5:
        g.drawString("Close the browser window to stop
        execution!", 70, 150);
        break;
default:
        g.drawString("Incorrect choice - please enter 1 - 5",
        70, 170);
        break;
    }
}
```

1. The keyword switch is followed by your input variable, number. Number contains the user's menu selection. What does the switch keyword do with the value in the number variable?

_____

_____

2. Explain why braces enclose all the case options.

_____

3. Explain the purpose of the case labels. (Note the colon, instead of the semicolon, at the end of each case label. This is the proper syntax for the case label line. Also note that the lines to be performed, dependent on the case, *do* end with a semicolon.)

_____

_____

4. Default is a special case. Explain the purpose of the default case.

_____

_____

One last thing to notice is the default case section of the switch structure. The braces required by compound command lines used in the if/else structure are not required in the case of a switch structure.

Now that you have used all three selection structures with your menu, there's one last question that needs to be answered.

5. Which of the three selection structures is the most appropriate to use with a menu? Why?

_____

_____

_____

_____

P R O J E C T   4 - 4 : Branching Off of Your Menu   Ⓑ

Now you're going to code a project that will allow you to "branch" off of a menu. However, you will be returning to the use of GUI controls instead of using a text-based menu.

In this project, you will add five buttons to your applet that will take the place of the text menu choices. As each button is clicked, something should happen—usually designated by the caption displayed on the button. You will code one of the buttons here and add the functionality to the others later.

You will also be shown how to take control of the layout of your GUI controls. In Lesson 2 you were introduced to the GridLayout method. In this project you will be introduced to the setLayout(null) method that will transfer layout control to you. This form of the method eliminates the use of any layout manager. Because of this you will be introduced to the setBounds method for placement of your controls. In addition, you will use the hide and show methods to further dictate when your controls appear.

Your output in this project will use the showStatus method. This method will display a string message in the *status window,* usually located at the lower left corner of the applet or browser window.

Step 1: Start Your Compiler

Start your compiler if it is not already running.

Step 2: Type in Your Code

Your code should be typed in exactly as follows. Save this program with the name **Proj4_4.java**. Remember to save your code after typing in the first line or two of your program, and then as often as possible thereafter.

```
// Proj4_4

// The classes from which your class will inherit
import java.awt.*;
import java.applet.*;
import java.awt.event.*;


// Your class definition
public class Proj4_4 extends Applet implements ActionListener
{
    // The control variables your program will use
    Button choice1, choice2, choice3, choice4;
    Label lblFirst, lblLast, lblEmail;
    TextField txtFirst, txtLast, txtEmail;

    // The initialization procedure for your applet
    public void init()
    {
        // This removes control from the layout manager and gives it
        // to the programmer.
        setLayout(null);

        // Adding each of the buttons and
        // adding an action listener to each one.
        // setBounds will set specific positions for the controls.
        choice1 = new Button("Add Record");
        choice1.setBounds(30, 30, 100, 30);
        add(choice1);
        choice1.addActionListener(this);

        // The action listeners are "commented out" since they are not
        // used until a later project.
        choice2 = new Button("Modify Record");
        choice2.setBounds(150, 30, 100, 30);
        //choice2.addActionListener(this);
        add(choice2);

        choice3 = new Button("Delete Record");
        choice3.setBounds(280, 30, 100, 30);
        //choice3.addActionListener(this);
        add(choice3);

        choice4 = new Button("View/Print Record");
        choice4.setBounds(410, 30, 100, 30);
        //choice4.addActionListener(this);
        add(choice4);

        // The controls are added, then hidden, until they are to
        // be used.
        lblFirst = new Label("First Name:");
        lblFirst.setBounds(30, 90, 100, 15);
```

```
            add(lblFirst);
            lblFirst.hide();

            txtFirst = new TextField(30);
            txtFirst.setBounds(150, 90, 150, 20);
            add(txtFirst);
            txtFirst.hide();

            lblLast = new Label("Last Name:");
            lblLast.setBounds(30, 120, 100, 15);
            add(lblLast);
            lblLast.hide();

            txtLast = new TextField(30);
            txtLast.setBounds(150, 120, 150, 20);
            add(txtLast);
            txtLast.hide();

            lblEmail = new Label("Email:");
            lblEmail.setBounds(30, 150, 100, 15);
            add(lblEmail);
            lblEmail.hide();

            txtEmail = new TextField(30);
            txtEmail.setBounds(150, 150, 150, 20);
            add(txtEmail);
            txtEmail.addActionListener(this);
            txtEmail.hide();

    }

    public void actionPerformed(ActionEvent e)
    {
            // A simple if structure is used to demonstrate "branching"
            // from a choice.
            if (e.getSource() == choice1)
            {
                lblFirst.show();
                txtFirst.show();
                lblLast.show();
                txtLast.show();
                lblEmail.show();
                txtEmail.show();

                // The status area of the applet is used to display the
                // message instead of the paint().
                showStatus("This choice would add a new record.");
            }

    }

}
```

Step 3: Save Your Program

Once you have finished typing in your code, save your code one final time before compiling your program.

Step 4: Compile and Run

Enter the commands necessary to compile and run your program. If errors occur during the compile, check your code, correct any errors, and rerun the program.

Step 5: Review Your Code

1. Explain the use of the following variables:

```
Button choice1, choice2, choice3, choice4;
Label lblFirst, lblLast, lblEmail;
TextField txtFirst, txtLast, txtEmail;
```

_____

_____

_____

_____

_____

_____

2. Explain the setLayout(null) method.

_____

_____

_____

_____

3. Explain the following block of code that adds one of the buttons:

```
choice1 = new Button("Add Record");
choice1.setBounds(30, 30, 100, 30);
add(choice1);
choice1.addActionListener(this);
```

_____

_____

_____

_____

4. Explain the parameters in the setBounds method.

```
choice2.setBounds(150, 30, 100, 30);
```

_____

5. Explain the relationship of the setBounds parameters *between* all the controls.

6. Explain the hide method used in the following block of code:

```
lblFirst = new Label("First Name:");
lblFirst.setBounds(30, 90, 100, 15);
add(lblFirst);
lblFirst.hide();
```

7. When does the following block of code actually execute?

```
public void actionPerformed(ActionEvent e)
{
   // A simple if structure is used to demonstrate "branching"
   // from a choice.
   if (e.getSource() == choice1)
   {
        lblFirst.show();
        txtFirst.show();
        lblLast.show();
        txtLast.show();
        lblEmail.show();
        txtEmail.show();
```

8. Explain the block of code shown in Question 7.

9. Explain the following method:

```
showStatus("This choice would add a new record.");
```

_____

_____

_____

_____

_____

10. Which selection structure is used in the applet? Is it appropriate? Why or why not?

_____

_____

_____

_____

_____

_____

_____

Step 6: Test Your Program

Run your program and see what happens when you choose choice 1, _Add A New Record_. The controls you will need to add a new record "show" when the button is clicked and you receive the showStatus message in the status window.

You'll notice that the other buttons do nothing. When you click them, nothing happens. You will add the functionality to these in a later project.

You now have an applet that lets the user choose what they would like to have happen.

PROJECT 4-5: Fancy Branching

You will continue to branch off of a menu in this project. However, you will be branching to separate calculations instead of branching to separate menu screens.

In this project, you will give the user the option of three calculations through the use of buttons. As each button is clicked, the user will be presented with a different set of controls. You will be using the same controls for each calculation; however, you will code the controls so that they prompt the user for the appropriate information.

8 6

The code used in this project comes from Proj3_1.java, Proj3_2.java, and Proj3_5.java. You may want to print out the code from these three projects, compare it to the code presented in Step 2, and then cut and paste the necessary code into this project.

The control structure that makes this project work is the selection structure. In this particular project you will use the if structure. At the end of this lesson you will modify this applet so that it uses the switch structure.

Your output in this project will once again use the showStatus method. This method will display a string message in the *status window,* usually located at the lower left corner of the applet or browser window.

Step 1: Start Your Compiler

Start your compiler if it is not already running.

Step 2: Type in Your Code

Your code should be typed in exactly as follows. Save this program with the name **Proj4_5.java**. Remember to save your code after typing in the first line or two of your program, and then as often as possible thereafter.

```java
// Proj4_5

// These are the classes needed for the applet to execute properly
import java.awt.*;
import java.applet.*;
import java.awt.event.*;

// This is the class definition
public class Proj4_5 extends Applet implements ActionListener
{

    // These are the controls to be used.
    // The labels and text fields are defined generically
    // because each choice will utilize the same labels
    // and text fields.
    Button button1, button2, button3, button4, button5, button6;
    Label label1, label2, label3;
    TextField text1, text2, text3;

    // These are the variables needed for this applet
    // from Proj3_3
    Float dollars1, xRate1;
    float forgnCurr1;

    // These are the variables needed for this applet
    // from Proj3_2
    Float forgnCurr2, xRate2;
    float dollars2;

    // These are the variables needed for this applet
    // from Proj3_5
    Float principal, intRate, months;
    double period, payment;
```

```
        // This code executes when the applet initializes
        public void init()
        {
                // This gives the programmer "control" over placement
                // of the applet controls.
                setLayout(null);

                // Six buttons with action listeners attached are added to the
applet.
                // The controls are set to specific positions with setBounds.
                button1 = new Button("$ To Foreign Currency");
                button1.setBounds(30, 30, 150, 30);
                add(button1);
                button1.addActionListener(this);

                button2 = new Button("Foreign Currency To $");
                button2.setBounds(200, 30, 150, 30);
                add(button2);
                button2.addActionListener(this);

                button3 = new Button("Simple Loan");
                button3.setBounds(370, 30, 150, 30);
                add(button3);
                button3.addActionListener(this);

                button4 = new Button("Convert $");
                button4.setBounds(30, 240, 150, 30);
                add(button4);
                button4.addActionListener(this);
                button4.hide();

                button5 = new Button("Convert Foreign Currency");
                button5.setBounds(200, 240, 150, 30);
                add(button5);
                button5.addActionListener(this);
                button5.hide();

                button6 = new Button("Calculate Repayment");
                button6.setBounds(370, 240, 150, 30);
                add(button6);
                button6.addActionListener(this);
                button6.hide();

                // The labels and text fields are added then hidden.
                // They will be made visible when used.
                label1 = new Label();
                label1.setBounds(30, 90, 150, 15);
                add(label1);
                label1.hide();

                text1 = new TextField(10);
                text1.setBounds(180, 90, 150, 20);
                add(text1);
                text1.hide();
```

```
        label2 = new Label();
        label2.setBounds(30, 120, 150, 15);
        add(label2);
        label2.hide();

        text2 = new TextField(10);
        text2.setBounds(180, 120, 150, 20);
        add(text2);
        text2.hide();

        label3 = new Label();
        label3.setBounds(30, 150, 150, 15);
        add(label3);
        label3.hide();

        text3 = new TextField(10);
        text3.setBounds(180, 150, 150, 20);
        add(text3);
        text3.hide();
    }

    // These lines of code are performed when the buttons are clicked.
    public void actionPerformed(ActionEvent e)
    {
        // The portion of the applet that gets performed is
        // coded within this if structure.
        if (e.getSource() == button1)
        {
            label1.setText("Amount in $:");
            label1.show();
            text1.show();

            label2.setText("Foreign Currency Name:");
            label2.show();
            text2.show();

            label3.setText("Exchange Rate:");
            label3.show();
            text3.show();

            button4.show();
            button5.hide();
            button6.hide();
        }

        if (e.getSource() == button2)
        {
            label1.setText("Amount in Foreign Currency:");
            label1.show();
            text1.show();

            label2.setText("Foreign Currency Name:");
            label2.show();
            text2.show();
```

```
                label3.setText("Exchange Rate:");
                label3.show();
                text3.show();

                button5.show();
                button6.hide();
                button4.hide();
        }

        if (e.getSource() == button3)
        {
                label1.setText("Amount borrowed:");
                label1.show();
                text1.show();

                label2.setText("Interest rate (x.xx):");
                label2.show();
                text2.show();

                label3.setText("Months borrowed:");
                label3.show();
                text3.show();

                button6.show();
                button4.hide();
                button5.hide();
        }

        if (e.getSource() == button4)
        {
                dollars1 = Float.valueOf(text1.getText());
                text2.getText();
                xRate1 = Float.valueOf(text3.getText());
                forgnCurr1 = dollars1.floatValue() * xRate1.floatValue();

                showStatus("This amount of dollars converts to " +
forgnCurr1 + " " + text2.getText() + ".");
        }

        if (e.getSource() == button5)
        {
                forgnCurr2 = Float.valueOf(text1.getText());
                text2.getText();
                xRate2 = Float.valueOf(text3.getText());
                dollars2 = forgnCurr2.floatValue() * xRate2.floatValue();

                showStatus("This amount of " + text2.getText() + " converts
to " + dollars2 + " dollars.");
        }

        if (e.getSource() == button6)
        {
                principal = Float.valueOf(text1.getText());
                intRate = Float.valueOf(text2.getText());
```

```
            months = Float.valueOf(text3.getText());

            period = months.floatValue() * 30/365;
            payment = principal.floatValue() + (principal.floatValue()
*((intRate.floatValue() / 100) * period));

            showStatus("The total amount you will owe is " + payment +
".");
        }
    }

}
```

Step 3: Save Your Program

Once you have finished typing in your code, save it one final time before compiling your program.

 **HOT TIP**

You may need to adjust the applet height and width values when running applets with an HTML page.

Step 4: Compile and Run

Enter the commands necessary to compile and run your program. If errors occur during the compile, check your code, correct any errors, and rerun the program.

Step 5: Review Your Code

1. Explain the use of the following variables:

```
Button button1, button2, button3, button4, button5, button6;
Label label1, label2, label3;
TextField text1, text2, text3;
```

_____

_____

_____

_____

_____

_____

2. Explain the setLayout(null) method.

_____

_____

_____

_____

3. Explain the following block of code that adds one of the buttons:

```
button1 = new Button("Foreign Currency To $");
button1.setBounds(30, 30, 150, 30);
add(button1);
button1.addActionListener(this);
```

_____

4. Explain the parameters in the setBounds method.

```
button1.setBounds(30, 30, 150, 30);
```

_____

_____

_____

_____

5. Explain the hide method used in the following block of code:

```
label1 = new Label();
label1.setBounds(30, 90, 150, 15);
add(label1);
label1.hide();
```

_____

_____

_____

_____

_____

6. When does the following block of code actually execute?

```
public void actionPerformed(ActionEvent e)
{
    // The portion of the applet that gets performed is
    // coded within this if structure.
    if (e.getSource() == button1)
    {
        label1.setText("Amount in $:");
        label1.show();
        text1.show();

        label2.setText("Foreign Currency Name:");
        label2.show();
        text2.show();

        label3.setText("Exchange Rate:");
        label3.show();
        text3.show();

        button4.show();
        button5.hide();
        button6.hide();
    }
```

_____

_____

_____

7. Explain the block of code shown in Question 6.

_____

_____

_____

_____

_____

_____

8. Explain the following method:

```
showStatus("The total amount you will owe is " + payment + ".");
```

_____

_____

_____

_____

_____

9. Which selection structure is used in the applet? Is it appropriate? Why or why not?

_____

_____

_____

_____

10. Explain why you needed to use the floatValue and valueOf methods in your calculations.

_____

_____

_____

_____

11. Explain why specific names are not given to the Label and TextField variables.

_____

_____

_____

_____

_____

_____

12. Explain why you initially hide the Label and TextField variables.

_____

_____

_____

_____

13. Explain why buttons 4, 5, and 6 were hidden.

_____

_____

_____

_____

14. Explain the following block of code. Why is it necessary?

```
button4.show();
button5.hide();
button6.hide();
```

_____

_____

_____

_____

_____

Step 6: Testing Your Program

Run your program and test each button. Do they perform the actions that you expect? Are the answers they provide correct? Remember—you have the original applets in your Lesson 3 projects. Compare the answers!

You now have an applet that lets the user choose what they would like to have happen, and you have an applet that combines multiple calculations.

Summary

Control structures are a very important part of programming. They allow you to organize programs and to provide control as to the function of the program. They let you provide the user with options and then control how the options are performed. This lesson contained sequence and selection structures.

Sequence is simply programming in a top-down structured manner, which Java uses both by default and within methods. Selection provides users with the ability to choose the functions they would like to perform. It provides the programmer with a way to give users choices while maintaining control over what happens when they make those choices. Review your code to look for the following: giving users a range of choices and then having many instructions performed for users "behind the scenes." This is "control," and it occurs in every program.

In this lesson, you also explored the if, if/else, and switch selection structures. The if structure is the simplest. If a condition is true, then something happens. And multiple if statements can be linked together. As mentioned earlier in this lesson, each if statement is tested. Even if the first one is found to be true, the others are tested. This doesn't matter in small programs, but it will in larger ones.

You learned that if/else structures are more efficient than the if statements alone, because once one is found to be true the others are ignored. Another difference between the two structures is the number of choices to be made. The if statement is probably more suitable for a simple two-choice selection, whereas the if/else structure is ideal for multiple selections. You can also link multiple if/else statements and can include multiple commands under each one. Just remember that braces {} must surround multiple commands under each if/else statement.

The last selection structure is the switch. The switch is neat, organized, and efficient. Although it requires extra commands (case, default, break) and you need to be careful about the syntax (case 'C':), the switch structure is much more organized. As with the if/else structure, once a correct case is encountered, the comparisons stop. But unlike the situation with if/else, multiple commands do not need to be placed in braces.

You now have additional tools at your beck and call that can be used to add selection control to your applets.

LESSON 4 REVIEW QUESTIONS

SHORT ANSWER

Define the following in the space provided.

1. if

_____

_____

2. if/else

_____

_____

3. switch

_____

_____

4. Functionality

_____

_____

5. Control structures

_____

_____

6. Sequence

_____

_____

7. Selection

_____

_____

8. Repetition

_____

_____

9. Decision making

_____

_____

10. Nested

_____

_____

11. while

_____

_____

12. Case

_____

_____

13. Break

_____

_____

14. else

_____

_____

15. Default

_____

_____

WRITTEN QUESTIONS

Write your answers to the following questions in the space provided.

1. Why do you use control structures?

_____

_____

2. Explain the importance of decision making in your programs.

_____

_____

3. Explain the difference between the if, if/else, and switch selection structures.

_____

_____

_____

_____

_____

4. Give an appropriate example of where to use each of the selection structures.

_____

_____

_____

_____

5. Write one if/else statement and one switch case statement that performs compound commands. Explain the difference in the syntax.

_____

_____

_____

_____

_____

_____

_____

_____

_____

6. Explain the setLayout(null) method used in this lesson.

_____

_____

7. Explain why the setBounds method needs to be used with controls if the setLayout(null) method is used.

_____

_____

8. Explain the showStatus method.

_____

_____

9. Explain the hide and show methods.

_____

_____

10. Explain the setText method.

_____

_____

TESTING YOUR SKILLS

⏱ **Estimated Time:**

Application 4-1 2 hours
Application 4-2 1 ¹/₂ hours
Application 4-3 1 ¹/₂ hours

APPLICATION 4-1

Open **Proj4_4.java** and add code for the remaining four buttons.

1. Design your various screen layouts on a piece of paper. Remember—you have modify, delete, view/print, and exit buttons to code.

2. Code the design to the screen layout. Do not initially add the code that will cause your program to branch to the actual routines or functions. Instead, display the screen and possibly an output line that shows that your selection structure works.

3. Continue using the if structure.

4. Compile and run your applet.

5. Save the modified code as **App4_1.java**.

APPLICATION 4-2

Open **App4_1.java** and replace the `if` structure with a switch structure.

1. Print out the code for App4_1.java.

2. Write the proper code for the switch structure that will replace your if structure.

3. Remember that the `switch` structure tests for an integer. Convert the user's choice into an int.

4. Use a break statement to separate each case.

5. Compile and run your applet.

6. Save the modified code as **App4_2.java**.

APPLICATION 4-3

Open **Proj4_5.java** and replace the if structure with a switch structure.

1. Print out the code for Proj4_5.java.

2. Write the proper code for the switch structure that will replace your if structure.

3. Remember that the switch structure tests for an integer. Convert the user's choice into an int.

4. Use a break statement to separate each case.

5. Compile and run your applet.

6. Save the modified code as **App4_3.java**.

SCANS

Design an applet that will allow a user to choose between multiple calculations, similar to Project 4-5. However, use the calculations from Lesson 3 that were not used in any of the projects in this lesson. Those are:

Project 3-1: Decimal to hexadecimal, octal, and binary conversion

Project 3-4: Height conversion—feet and inches to centimeters and meters

Either create a brand new applet that uses these two calculations or add these two calculations to **Proj4_5.java.**

REPETITIONS

OBJECTIVES

On completion of this lesson, you should be able to:

- Demonstrate the use of repetition control structures.

- Discriminate between the use of the while, do/while, and for repetition structures.

- Design code that utilizes the three repetition structures.

- Revise earlier projects by integrating repetition structures.

- Analyze your programs to determine their correctness.

 Estimated Time: 5 ½ hours

Introduction

One of the strengths of computers is their ability to perform calculations at a tremendously fast speed. Because of their ability, it makes sense to let them perform calculations that would take human beings a great deal of time to finish. These calculations must often be performed repeatedly to arrive at the correct answer, such as in the case of compound interest. That is why ***repetition control structures*** are used.

Repetition control structures allow you to add ***looping*** to your programs. Looping simply means that a sequence of code is repeated over and over, until a condition is met. However, there is a danger with repetition control structures that the looping will get out of hand and create an "endless" loop. This means that you have provided a condition, or coded your logic wrong, so that the ending condition will never be met.

You'll find that repetition is very useful in the programs you write. The way most programs you have written execute is that the user enters one record and then the program ends. To input another record, the program must run again. This is not very efficient. It makes more sense to let the user enter records until he or she is finished. In Java applets this is not a problem since the applet is always "on" until the browser window is closed. However, Java applets are only one type of program.

As mentioned in Lesson 4, there are seven types of control structures that are grouped into three categories: ***sequence***, ***selection***, and ***repetition***. This lesson covers the repetition category.

There are three repetition control structures, ***while, do/while,*** and ***for.*** The differences between the three are subtle but necessary to understand. The ***while*** structure is built on the premise that the commands in the body of the structure will continue to execute "while" some condition is true. When the condition becomes false, the while structure releases control and executes the next line after the structure. The condition is tested for at the beginning of the structure. This means that there is a possibility that the while structure may not even be entered if the condition is not met. Also, note that the commands in the body of the while structure must be surrounded by braces.

In a do/while structure, the commands are executed until the while condition becomes false; however, the while condition is tested for after the command(s) executes. This means that the commands will execute *at least once*. This is very useful if the user chooses to do something but only needs to perform the action one time. The commands in the do/while structure are also enclosed in braces; however, the commands are part of the do section of the structure.

Last but not least is the for structure. The syntax of this structure is slightly more complicated, but easy to understand once you see it. The for structure uses a **counter** to control repetition. The format of the for structure causes a counter to be initialized to a specific value, a condition for the counter to be measured against is then created, and then an action takes place, usually an **increment** of the counter. The following is an example of the for structure:

```
for ( int counter =1; counter <= 10; counter++)
        g.drawstring("This is a for loop!", xpos, ypos);
```

In this example, the variable counter is initialized to the number 1. This loop will execute as long as the counter is less than or equal to 10, and after each loop the counter will be incremented by 1 after the command executes. By placing this structure in a program, you will get a screen filled with 10 separate lines of "This is a for structure." You will get the opportunity to code all three structures plus some variations. This lesson will focus on the following:

- **Understanding control structures and the use of repetition control structures.** You will learn about repetition control structures and understand when and how to apply them, as well as exploring other types of control structures.

- **Learning when to use the while, the do/while, and the for repetition structures and designing code that utilizes each.** You will learn the appropriate use of the three repetition structures, and you will be given the opportunity to design the code necessary to make them work.

- **Revising earlier projects by integrating repetition structures.** You will modify code you've already created by integrating repetition structures.

- **Analyzing your programs to determine their correctness.** This part of programming never ends. The bottom line is that your programs must work properly. If you continue to develop your understanding of Java by constantly analyzing your programs, you will be the better for it in the long run because you will have developed good work habits!

So, get out your hula hoops and get ready to loop!

PROJECT 5-1:
Simple Repetition Overview—For Loop

You will program an applet built around the for loop example provided in the introduction.

Step 1: Start Your Compiler

Start your compiler if it is not already running.

Step 2: Type Code for the *for* Structure

Your code should be typed in exactly as follows. Save the program as **Proj5_1.java**. Remember to save your code after typing in the first line or two of your program, and then as often as possible thereafter.

```
// Proj5_1

// These are the classes needed for this applet to execute.

import java.awt.Graphics;
import java.applet.Applet;

// This is your class definition.

public class Proj5_1 extends Applet
{

    public void paint (Graphics g)
    {
        // These are the position variables for g.drawstring.
        int xpos = 20, ypos = 20;

        // Everything else we need is included in the for loop.
        // Don't forget the braces for the body of code.
        for (int counter = 1; counter <=10; counter++){
            g.drawString ("This is a for structure.", xpos, ypos);
            xpos += 5;
            ypos += 5;
        }
    }
}
```

Step 3: Save Your Program

Once you have finished typing in your code, save the code one final time before compiling your program.

Step 4: Compile and Run

Enter the commands necessary to compile and run your program. If errors occur during the compile, check your code, correct any errors, and rerun the program.

You should have 10 lines of "This is a for structure." displayed in your applet.

Step 5: Review Your Code

1. Explain what happens when these two lines of code are executed:

```
for (int counter = 1; counter <=10; counter++){
    g.drawString ("This is a for structure.", xpos, ypos);
```

_____

_____

103

2. Explain why the clauses enclosed in the parentheses in the `for` line are separated by semicolons.

_____

_____

3. Explain the significance of using `counter <= 10` versus using `counter < 11`.

_____

_____

_____

4. Explain the use of the `xpos` and `ypos` integer variables.

_____

_____

_____

5. Explain `counter++`.

_____

_____

_____

_____

6. Explain `xpos += 5` and `ypos += 5`.

_____

_____

_____

_____

You now have a quick, but efficient, example of a for loop.

PROJECT 5-2:
Simple Repetition Overview—While Structure Ⓑ

You will program an applet that replaces the `for` loop in Proj5_1.java with a `while` structure.

Step 1: Start Your Compiler

Start your compiler if it is not already running. Open **Proj5_1.java**.

Step 2: Print Your Code

Print the code from **Proj5_1.java**. It will be easier to complete this project by having a hard copy of the code to which you can refer. Your code should look like the following:

```java
// Proj5_1

// These are the classes needed for this applet to execute.

import java.awt.Graphics;
import java.applet.Applet;

// This is your class definition.

public class Proj5_1 extends Applet
{

    public void paint (Graphics g)
    {
            // These are the position variables for g.drawstring.
            int xpos = 20, ypos = 20;

            // Everything else we need is included in the for loop.
            // Don't forget the braces for the body of code.
            for (int counter = 1; counter <= 10; counter++){
                    g.drawString ("This is a for structure.", xpos, ypos);
                    xpos += 5;
                    ypos += 5;
            }
    }
}
```

If your code does not look like this, make the necessary modifications and then save your program. After saving the program, compile and run it, correcting any errors necessary in order for it to run properly. Save the program one final time. Then print out a hard copy.

Step 3: Convert Your For Loop to a While Structure

These two loops are very similar. However, the for loop initializes its counter within itself, but the while structure must have the counter initialized outside of its structure.

1. In the space below, write the code for the while structure. Save your modified code as **Proj5_2.java**.

_____

_____

_____

_____

_____

_____

_____

_____

_____

_____

_____

_____

_____

Step 4: Compile and Run

Enter the commands necessary to compile and run your program. If errors occur during the compile, check your code, correct any errors, and rerun the program. You should have 10 lines of "This is a while structure." displayed in your applet.

Step 5: Review Your Code

Your code should look similar to the following:

```
// Proj5_2

// These are the classes needed for this applet to execute.

import java.awt.Graphics;
import java.applet.Applet;

// This is your class definition.

public class Proj5_2 extends Applet
{

    public void paint (Graphics g)
    {
        // These are the position variables for g.drawstring
        // and the counter for the while loop.
        int xpos = 20, ypos = 20, counter = 1;

        // Everything else we need is included in the while loop.
        // Don't forget the braces for the body of code.
        while (counter <= 10){
            g.drawString ("This is a while structure.", xpos, ypos);
            xpos += 5;
            ypos += 5;
            counter++;
        }
    }
}
```

1. Explain what happens when this block of code is executed:

```
        while (counter <= 10){
            g.drawString ("This is a while structure.", xpos, ypos);
            xpos += 5;
            ypos += 5;
            counter++;
        }
```

106

2. Explain why the body of the while structure is enclosed in braces.

3. Explain the significance of using `counter <= 10` versus using `counter < 11`.

4. Explain the use of the xpos and ypos integer variables.

5. Explain counter++.

PROJECT 5-3:
Simple Repetition Overview—Do/While Structure

Ⓑ

You will program an applet that replaces the while loop in Proj5_2.java with a do/while structure.

Step 1: Start Your Compiler

Start your compiler if it is not already running. Open **Proj5_2.java**.

Step 2: Print Your Code

Print the code from Proj5_2.java. It will be easier to complete this project by having a hard copy of the code to which you can refer. Your code should look like the following:

```
// Proj5_2

// These are the classes needed for this applet to execute.

import java.awt.Graphics;
```

```java
import java.applet.Applet;

// This is your class definition.

public class Proj5_2 extends Applet
{

    public void paint (Graphics g)
    {
            // These are the position variables for g.drawstring
            // and the counter for the while loop.
            int xpos = 20, ypos = 20, counter = 1;

            // Everything else we need is included in the while loop.
            // Don't forget the braces for the body of code.
            while (counter <= 10){
                    g.drawString ("This is a while structure.", xpos, ypos);
                    xpos += 5;
                    ypos += 5;
                    counter++;
            }
    }
}
```

If your code does not look like this, make the necessary modifications and then save the program. After saving the program, compile and run it, correcting any errors necessary in order for it to run properly. Save the program one final time. Then print a hard copy.

Step 3: Convert Your For Loop to a Do/While Structure

These two loops are very similar. However, the while structure tests its condition at the beginning of the loop, but the do/while structure does not test its condition until after the loop. This means that the while loop may never execute, whereas the do/while loop will at least execute once.

1. In the space below, write the code for the do/while structure. Save your modified code as **Proj5_3.java**.

_____

_____

_____

_____

_____

_____

_____

_____

_____

_____

Step 4: Compile and Run

Enter the commands necessary to compile and run your program. If errors occur during the compile, check your code, correct any errors, and rerun the program. You should have 10 lines of "This is a do/while structure." displayed in your applet.

Step 5: Review Your Code

Your code should look similar to the following:

```
// Proj5_3

// These are the classes needed for this applet to execute.

import java.awt.Graphics;
import java.applet.Applet;

// This is your class definition.

public class Proj5_3 extends Applet
{

    public void paint (Graphics g)
    {
            // These are the position variables for g.drawstring
            // and the counter for the do while loop.
            int xpos = 20, ypos = 20, counter = 1;

            // Everything else we need is included in the do while loop.
            // Don't forget the braces for the body of code.
            do {
                    g.drawString ("This is a do/while structure.", xpos, ypos);
                    xpos += 5;
                    ypos += 5;
                    counter++;
            } while (counter <= 10);
    }
}
```

1. Explain what happens when this block of code is executed:

```
do {
        g.drawString ("This is a do/while structure.", xpos, ypos);
        xpos += 5;
        ypos += 5;
        counter++;
} while (counter <= 10);
```

_____

_____

2. Explain why the body of the do/while structure is enclosed in braces.

_____

_____

3. Explain the significance of using `counter <= 10` versus using `counter < 11`.

_____

_____

_____

4. Explain the use of the xpos and ypos integer variables.

_____

_____

_____

_____

5. Explain `counter++`.

_____

_____

_____

_____

6. Will the do/while loop always execute at least once? Explain.

_____

_____

_____

PROJECT 5-4 : Compound Interest

In previous lessons, you coded programs that deal with computing interest for short periods of time. You even modified these programs to calculate simple interest over a period of years, although interest is normally compounded when someone borrows, or invests, money for more than a year. Now you're going to actually compound interest on your long-term investments the way it's supposed to be done.

Step 1: Start Your Compiler

If your compiler is not already running, start it now.

Step 2: Design Your Program

You know you'll need a class. You will also need some variables of a type that can be used for math calculations. And, since compounding means to add interest upon interest, the program must contain a repetition structure.

1. In the space below, write the code needed for the class while leaving space for the additional code you will need. Make sure you include the classes from which you will need to inherit.

_____

_____

_____

_____

_____

_____

_____

_____

_____

_____

_____

_____

_____

_____

_____

2. Add in the variables you will need for your calculation. You know you'll need a variable for principal, interest rate, and years. These variables will get their values from text fields. And each text field will need a label. You can assume that interest will compound monthly. Therefore, if you are borrowing for a period of years, you'll need to convert years into months. And you will need to convert the annual interest rate into a monthly interest rate. Then you'll need to convert the interest rate into a decimal. So, you will need at least five variables. However, you may need more. **REMEMBER:** Some of your data types may be Java objects, while some may be primitive data types. Conversions between the two will need to take place. Write down the variable names and types that you will be using.

_____

_____

_____

_____

_____

_____

_____

Step 3: Type in Your Code

Type in the code as you've written it so far. Save the program as **Proj5_4.java**. **REMEMBER:** Save often as you type in the code. Add comments to your code as you enter it.

Step 4: Design Your Repetition Structure

You know that you will need to compute interest each and every month for which your money will be invested. Therefore, you know you will have a fixed number of repetitions.

1. Which repetition structure does that suggest? Explain your answer.

_____

_____

_____

You also know that your answer will need to be reused each time you add interest. This may suggest a slightly different assignment operator.

2. Code your repetition structure. Remember to add the additional variable to your variable list and to your code. Design your repetition structure below.

_____

_____

_____

_____

_____

_____

_____

_____

Step 5: Type in Your Code

Type in the additional code you've written. Remember to save the program often as you type in the code. Add comments to your code as you enter it.

Step 6: Save Your Program

When you have finished typing the code, save your program once more before moving on to the next step.

Step 7: Compile and Run

Enter the commands necessary to compile and run your program. If errors occur during the compile, check your code, correct any errors, and rerun the program.

Remember to save your program any time you make changes!

Test your program by computing the answer to your investment with a calculator. The basic formula for compounded interest is as follows:

```
Total = principal + (principal x the interest rate per period)
```

Then move your total amount back into principal and perform the calculation again. The calculation is looped for the total number of months for which you've invested your money.

You now have a program that provides a useful calculation to your users. And it includes a repetition structure. Now they can figure out how much money they will make on their investments!

112

Step 8: Explain Your Program

If you are having major problems at this point, check your code against the code shown below.

```
// Proj5_4

// These are the classes needed for the applet to execute properly
import java.awt.*;
import java.applet.*;
import java.awt.event.*;

// This is the class definition
public class Proj5_4 extends Applet implements ActionListener
{
    // These are the variables needed for this applet
    Float principal, intRate, years;
    float original, periods, intPerPeriod, total;
    Label lblPrin, lblInterest, lblYears;
    TextField txtPrin, txtInterest, txtYears;

    // This code executes when the applet initializes
    public void init()
    {
        setLayout(null);

        // Three labels and three text fields are added to the applet
        lblPrin = new Label("Enter the amount you will invest: ");
        lblPrin.setBounds(30, 30, 250, 20);
        add(lblPrin);

        txtPrin = new TextField(10);
        txtPrin.setBounds(300, 30, 100, 20);
        add(txtPrin);

        lblInterest = new Label("Enter the interest % you will earn: ");
        lblInterest.setBounds(30, 60, 250, 20);
        add(lblInterest);

        txtInterest = new TextField(10);
        txtInterest.setBounds(300, 60, 100, 20);
        add(txtInterest);

        lblYears = new Label("Enter the # of years your money will be
invested: ");
        lblYears.setBounds(30, 90, 250, 20);
        add(lblYears);

        // The action listener is attached to the last text field
        txtYears = new TextField(10);
        txtYears.setBounds(300, 90, 100, 20);
        add(txtYears);
        txtYears.addActionListener(this);
    }
```

```
// These lines of code are performed when the Enter key is pressed
public void actionPerformed(ActionEvent e)
{
        principal = Float.valueOf(txtPrin.getText());
        original = principal.floatValue();
        total = principal.floatValue();
        intRate = Float.valueOf(txtInterest.getText());
        years = Float.valueOf(txtYears.getText());
        periods = years.floatValue() * 12;
        intPerPeriod = intRate.floatValue()/100/12;

        for (int counter = 1; counter <= periods; counter++)
            total += (total * intPerPeriod);
        repaint();
}

// The paint method displays the output
public void paint (Graphics g)
{
        g.drawString("Your investment of " + original + " will become " +
total + " in " + years + " years.", 30, 210);

}
}
```

Make sure you keep practicing your ability to analyze and explain Java code. Explain each line or block of code from your program in the space provided.

_____

_____

_____

_____

_____

_____

_____

_____

_____

_____

_____

_____

_____

_____

_____

_____

_____

114

_____

_____

_____

_____

_____

_____

_____

_____

_____

_____

_____

_____

_____

When you're finished, discuss your answers with your teacher and classmates to reinforce your ability to analyze Java code.

PROJECT 5-5:
While Structure with an Embedded Switch

The program you will code in this project deals with gathering survey results and then terminating the counting when the last item is entered. Such a test comes in handy when you are not sure how many items the user needs to input. You will handle this by prompting the user to input a zero when finished. When the user enters a zero, the while loop ends and then the totals from each category are displayed in the status window.

The basic structure of this test is to perform/execute commands until the user enters a zero. This logic suggests that you do not use the for repetition structure, since you do not know how many times you will need to loop. Therefore, you will use either the do/while or the while repetition structure.

You will enter survey results to be accumulated and then displayed to the screen. The participants in the survey were asked to agree, disagree, or offer no opinion to a question. The question was asked at a local mall to teenagers only. Since you had 24 students asking the question, you don't know how many responses to expect. All you know is that you have a huge pile of papers!

Step 1: Start Your Compiler

If your compiler is not already running, start it now.

Step 2: Design Your Program

1. In the space below, write the code needed for your program. (***HINT:*** Outline your class, set up the program flow, and create the variables. Prompt users to enter the information you need while making sure that they know about the "termination" option with which to end their input. If the user enters an incorrect choice, let him or her know it. Add up the survey results by response. Display the totals of each category on the screen.)

_____

_____

_____

_____

_____

_____

_____

_____

_____

_____

_____

_____

_____

_____

_____

_____

_____

_____

_____

_____

_____

_____

_____

_____

_____

_____

_____

_____

_____

_____

_____

_____

_____

_____

_____

_____

_____

Step 3: Type in Your Program

Type in the code as you create each section. Save the program as **Proj5_5.java**. *REMEMBER:* Save often as you type in the code. Add comments to your code as you enter it.

Step 4: Save Your Program

When you have finished typing the code, save your program once more before moving on to the next step.

Step 5: Compile and Run

Enter the commands necessary to compile and run your program. If errors occur during the compile, check your code, correct any errors, and rerun the program.

Remember to save your program any time you make changes!

When you run your program you will need to test the program for proper execution. This includes input options, switching and accumulating, repetition, and exiting the program.

Step 6: Explain Your Program

Make sure you keep practicing your ability to analyze and explain Java code. Explain each line or block of code from your program in the space provided.

_____

_____

_____

_____

_____

_____

_____

_____

_____

_____

_____

_____

_____

_____

_____

_____

_____

_____

_____

_____

_____

_____

_____

_____

_____

_____

_____

_____

_____

_____

_____

_____

_____

_____

_____

_____

_____

_____

_____

_____

_____

_____

When you're finished, discuss your answers with your teacher and classmates to reinforce your ability to analyze Java code.

If you are having major problems at this point, check your code against the code shown below.

```
// Proj5_5

// These are the classes needed for your applet to execute properly.
import java.awt.*;
import java.applet.*;
import java.awt.event.*;

// This is your class definition.
public class Proj5_5 extends Applet implements ActionListener
{
```

119

```
// Two labels will be used to prompt the user.
// One text field will be used for user input.
// The ints are for response accumulation and the while loop.
Label lblResponse1, lblResponse2;
TextField txtResponse;
int response, Acount, Dcount, NOcount;

// This code executes when the applet initializes.
public void init()
{
        // This gives layout control to the programmer.
        setLayout(null);

        // The labels and text field are being added.
        lblResponse1 = new Label("Enter the participant's response:");
        lblResponse1.setBounds(30, 30, 250, 20);
        add(lblResponse1);

        lblResponse2 = new Label("1 - Agree, 2 - Disagree, 3 - No Opinion,
Zero to End");
        lblResponse2.setBounds(30, 45, 250, 20);
        add(lblResponse2);

        txtResponse = new TextField(5);
        txtResponse.setBounds(300, 30, 50, 20);
        txtResponse.addActionListener(this);
        add(txtResponse);

}

public void actionPerformed(ActionEvent e)
{
        // The while loop is contingent on the user NOT entering zero.
        while ((response = Integer.parseInt(txtResponse.getText())) != 0)
        {
                // The block of code that executes is dependent on the
                   user's input.
                switch(response)
                {
                case 1:
                        ++Acount;
                        // This empties the text field after each response is
                         input.
                        txtResponse.setText("");
                        showStatus("Agree");
                        break;

                case 2:
                        ++Dcount;
                        txtResponse.setText("");
                        showStatus("Disagree");
                        break;
```

```
                        case 3:
                                ++NOcount;
                                txtResponse.setText("");
                                showStatus("No opinion");
                                break;

                        default:
                                showStatus("Enter a correct response!");
                                txtResponse.setText("");
                                break;
                        }
                }
                // This is the final tally of the user input.
                // It executes when the user terminates the while loop
                // by entering zero.
                // It also clears the text field.
                txtResponse.setText("");
                showStatus(Acount + " agree, " + Dcount + " disagree, " + " and "
+ NOcount + " have no opinion.");
        }
}
```

One thing that should be pointed out again in this switch selection structure is that the test is based on an integer. Therefore, the input from the user needs to be taken from the test field and "transformed" into an integer. This allows you to make the switch structure work.

You now have a program that allows the user to input an unknown amount of information because it tests for input termination. You can use this test with any of the programs you have developed that allow a variable amount of input. So go forth and integrate control structures where necessary into your code!

Summary

Control structures are a very important part of programming. In this lesson, you concentrated on repetition structures. You looped simple loops using the various repetition structures. This allowed you to sample the various types of repetition.

You also learned how to design calculations that need to repeat. One of the most obvious and useful calculations is the computation of compound interest. In earlier projects, you created programs that calculated simple interest. Compounding interest is a natural add-on to your collection of calculations! Since you knew, or at least could calculate from user-provided information, how many times the calculation needed to repeat, you used the for repetition structure.

The last project you created tested for a termination character. Such a structured program allows the user to control the amount of information being input. This project reinforced the while repetition structure and the switch selection structure.

Now you are capable of creating repetition structures so that you do not need to rerun the same program every time you switch from function to function. You should be getting a pretty good handle on integrated program design!

SHORT ANSWER

Define the following in the space provided.

1. while

_____

_____

2. do/while

_____

_____

3. for

_____

_____

4. Repetition control structure

_____

_____

5. Looping

_____

_____

6. do

_____

_____

7. counter

_____

_____

8. Increment

_____

_____

9. Postincrement

_____

_____

10. Preincrement

_____

_____

11. Break

_____

_____

12. Assignment operator

_____

_____

13. Endless loop

_____

_____

14. Integer.parseInt()

_____

_____

WRITTEN QUESTIONS

Write your answers to the following questions in the space provided.

1. Why are repetition control structures used?

_____

2. Explain the differences between the while and do/while repetition structures.

_____

_____

_____

_____

3. Explain the appropriate use of the for repetition structure.

_____

_____

4. Explain the difference between _preincrement_ and _postincrement._

_____

_____

5. Explain the use of the Integer.parseInt() function.

_____

_____

6. Explain how the user can control variable amounts of input.

_____

_____

_____

7. Explain the use of the counter in the for structure.

_____

_____

8. Explain the syntax of the for structure.

_____

_____

_____

9. Write two lines of code that increment a variable—one line for a preincrement, and one line for a postincrement.

_____

_____

TESTING YOUR SKILLS

Estimated Time:

Application 5-1 1 hour
Application 5-2 1 hour
Application 5-3 1 ¹/₂ hours

APPLICATION 5-1

Change the repetition structure in Project 5-4 to a while structure. Save your modified program as **App5_1.java**.

APPLICATION 5-2

Change the repetition structure in Project 5-4 to a do/while structure. Save your modified program as **App5_2.java**.

APPLICATION 5-3

Change the repetition and switch structures in Project 5-5 to an empty for loop—for (;;)—and an if/else selection structure. Save your modified program as **App5_3.java.**

CRITICAL THINKING Ⓐ

Estimated Time: 4 hours

Create a program that will average the grades you receive for your assignments during this grading period. Use a while structure that tests for a termination character, unless you know the exact number of graded assignments that you will have in this grading period. In that case, a for structure might work better.

While you're at it, add a selection structure that will take your average and assign a letter grade to it based on your school's grading system. Save this program with a meaningful .java filename.

ARRAYS

OBJECTIVES

On completion of this lesson, you should be able to:

- Explain arrays.

- Declare and initialize arrays.

- Display array output using graphic objects and the status window.

- Select array elements using subscripts.

- Set array size using a constant variable.

- Sort data in both ascending and descending order.

- Perform linear searches.

⏲ **Estimated Time: 10 hours**

Introduction

Data manipulation is a key part of computer programming. In fact, there are probably few, if any, application programs available that do not offer the user the choice of some sort of data manipulation. One of the most important aspects of data manipulation is the ability to store and retrieve information. In this lesson we will discuss temporary storage and data manipulation.

Arrays are a group of consecutive memory locations that all have the same name and same data type. They are useful for temporarily storing data to be manipulated. With arrays we can structure the data that is input, basically placing the data in "locations" within a "table." We can then access the data by explicitly going to its location using a subscript. A *subscript* is simply the number of the *element*, or item, in the array. Even though subscripts are simple, they can cause some confusion.

Arrays start numbering their elements, or items, with *zero*. So the first element in an array is *not* element 1, but element zero. So, if you are looking for the sixth item in the array, it would be subscript 5 (0, 1, 2, 3, 4, **5**). This confusion sometimes leads to *off-by-one errors*. If you want to display the contents of item 6, you need to ask for subscript 5. If you ask for subscript 6, you will actually get the seventh item in the array. One way to avoid this problem is to remember that every time you are looking for a specific element, the subscript becomes the element you are looking for *minus 1*.

Arrays are also useful in compiling results, such as you did with the simple survey created in Project 5-5, and in sorting data. This lesson will focus on the following:

- **Declaring and initializing arrays.** You will be creating arrays and showing various ways to initialize them.

- **Displaying array output using graphic objects and the status window.** You will be applying the same display techniques you have used in earlier projects to generate output in an easy, useful format.

- **Setting array size using a constant variable.** One of the best ways to initialize a variable is to use a *constant variable*. A constant variable lets you change the array size by changing the value of the constant variable. This method results in your programs being coded clearer and executing faster.

- **Selecting array elements using subscripts.** You will use explicit subscripts that refer to the exact number of the element in an array, and you will use a variable in place of the subscript. You will be shown situations where each is appropriate.

- **Sorting data in ascending and descending order.** *Sorting* data is very important in computer applications, especially in database activities. Data is usually stored in a computer in the order in which it is entered. You need to be able to reorder the data so that it is in a more logical sequence, depending on the application. For example, a personal phone book would be much easier to use if it were in alphabetic order by last name. We'll take a look at sorting data in both *ascending* and *descending* order.

- **Performing linear searches.** Searching for data is important, especially in the areas of database administration and Web site administration. Think about how much time you spend looking for things, and then think about how helpful it would be if you could create the ultimate search program!

PROJECT 6 - 1 : Simple Array Ⓑ

In this project, you will declare and initialize a simple array.

Step 1: Start Your Compiler

Start your compiler if it is not already running.

Step 2: Type in Your Code

Your code should be typed in exactly as follows. Save this program as **Proj6_1.java**. Remember to save your code after typing in the first line or two of your program, and then as often as possible thereafter.

```
// Proj6_1

// These are the classes needed for this applet to execute.

import java.awt.Graphics;
import java.applet.Applet;
```

```
// This is your class definition.

public class Proj6_1 extends Applet
{
   // This is the array declaration. The new command happens automatically.
   int simpleArray[] = {1, 3, 5, 7, 9, 11, 13, 15, 17, 19};

   public void paint (Graphics g)
   {
        // These are the position variables for g.drawstring.
        int xpos = 20, ypos = 20;

        // Everything else we need is included in the for loop.
        // Don't forget the braces for the body of code.
        for (int element = 0; element <= 10; element++){
             g.drawString ("Element # " + element + " holds the value " +
simpleArray[element] +".", xpos, ypos);
             ypos += 15;
        }
   }
}
```

Step 3: Save Your Program

Once you have finished typing in your code, save it one final time before compiling your program.

Step 4: Compile and Run

Enter the commands necessary to compile and run your program. If errors occur during the compile, check your code, correct any errors, and rerun the program.

You should have 10 lines displayed on your screen that look like the following:

```
Element #0 holds the value 1.
Element #1 holds the value 3.
Element #2 holds the value 5.
Element #3 holds the value 7.
Element #4 holds the value 9.
Element #5 holds the value 11.
Element #6 holds the value 13.
Element #7 holds the value 15.
Element #8 holds the value 17.
Element #9 holds the value 19.
```

Step 5: Explain Your Code

The above code is broken into blocks, which you are asked to explain below.

1. Explain the following line of code:

```
int simpleArray[] = {1, 3, 5, 7, 9, 11, 13, 15, 17, 19};
```

_____

_____

_____

_____

_____

_____

2. Explain the for statement in the following block of code:

```
for (int element = 0; element <= 10; element++){
        g.drawString ("Element # " + element + " holds the value " +
simpleArray[element] +".", xpos, ypos);
        ypos += 15;
 }
```

_____

_____

_____

3. Explain why the loop condition is less than or equal to 10.

_____

_____

_____

4. Explain the command performed each time through the for loop.

_____

_____

_____

5. What benefit does using the element variable provide?

_____

_____

_____

6. What are the following variables used for?

```
int xpos = 20, ypos = 20;
```

_____

_____

_____

PROJECT 6-2:
Initializing an Array from User Input

B

Arrays usually do not initialize themselves. Nor does the programmer initialize arrays. It is the user who determines which data needs to be in the array. In this project, you will create a loop that allows the user to input the numbers needed.

Step 1: Start Your Compiler

Start your compiler if it is not already running.

Step 2: Open the Project 6-1 File

Open your **Proj6_1.java** file, and save it as **Proj6_2.java**.

Step 3: Modify Your Code

Modify your code so that it looks exactly like the code shown below.

```
// Proj6_2

// These are the classes needed for your applet to execute properly.
import java.awt.*;
import java.applet.*;
import java.awt.event.*;

// This is your class definition.
public class Proj6_2 extends Applet implements ActionListener
{
    // One label will be used to prompt the user.
    // One text field will be used for user input.
    // The ints are for an array, a subscript, and a value holder.
    Label lblResponse1;
    TextField txtResponse;
    int element, value;
    int simpleArray[];

    // This code executes when the applet initializes.
    public void init()
    {
        // This gives layout control to the programmer.
        setLayout(null);
        // The following lines allocate memory to the array
        // and initialize the subscript.
        simpleArray = new int[10];
        element = 0;

        // The label and text field are being added.
        lblResponse1 = new Label("Enter 10 numbers:");
        lblResponse1.setBounds(30, 30, 250, 20);
        add(lblResponse1);

        txtResponse = new TextField(5);
```

129

```
        txtResponse.setBounds(300, 30, 50, 20);
        txtResponse.addActionListener(this);
        add(txtResponse);

    }

    // When the Enter key is pressed the value in the text field will
    // be assigned to the proper array element.
    public void actionPerformed(ActionEvent e)
    {
        if (element == 10)
            showStatus("This array only takes 10 numbers!");
        value = Integer.parseInt(txtResponse.getText());
        simpleArray[element] = value;
        element++;
        txtResponse.setText("");
        repaint();
    }

    public void paint (Graphics g)
    {
        // These are the position variables for g.drawstring.
        int xpos = 20, ypos = 80;

        // Everything else we need is included in the for loop.
        // Don't forget the braces for the body of code.
        for (int position = 0; position <= 10; position++){
            g.drawString ("Element # " + position + " holds the value "
+ simpleArray[position] +".", xpos, ypos);
            ypos += 15;
        }
    }
}
```

Step 4: Save Your Program

Once you have finished typing in your code, save it one final time before compiling your program.

Step 5: Compile and Run

Enter the commands necessary to compile and run your program. If errors occur during the compile, check your code, correct any errors, and rerun the program.

Your program should ask you for 10 numbers, although not specifically. After the 10th number is input, the program will quit accepting numbers, and you will get a message in the status window. The result is that you should have 10 lines displayed on your screen that look like the following. Of course, your values will differ depending on your input.

```
Element # 0 holds the value 1.

Element # 1 holds the value 2.

Element # 2 holds the value 3.

Element # 3 holds the value 4.
```

130

```
Element # 4 holds the value 5.

Element # 5 holds the value 6.

Element # 6 holds the value 7.

Element # 7 holds the value 8.

Element # 8 holds the value 9.

Element # 9 holds the value 10.
```

Have you noticed that this output is very similar to the output from Project 6-1? The only difference is that the user sets the values.

Step 6: Review Your Code

Now let's take a look at your modifications.

1. Explain the execution of the code shown and the purpose it serves:

```
public void actionPerformed(ActionEvent e)
{
        if (element == 10)
                showStatus("This array only takes 10 numbers!");
        value = Integer.parseInt(txtResponse.getText());
        simpleArray[element] = value;
        element++;
        txtResponse.setText("");
        repaint();
}
```

_____

_____

_____

_____

_____

_____

_____

_____

_____

2. Explain the use of the following variables in conjunction with the above block of code:

```
int element, value;
int simpleArray[];
```

_____

_____

_____

3. Explain how the following lines of code affect the included variables:

```
simpleArray = new int[10];
element = 0;
```

When you're finished, discuss your answers with your teacher and classmates to reinforce your ability to analyze Java code.

It's important to know how arrays can be initialized both by the programmer and by the user. The loop used in this project allows you to have the user input the data required.

P R O J E C T 6 - 3 :
Using a Constant Variable to Set Array Size

This project is short and sweet, but important! Constant variables can be used to initialize array size. By using a constant variable you can make your program much more scalable. If you would like an array size to increase from 10 to 350, or to 150,000, then you only need to change the value assigned to the constant variable. By using the constant variable in the remainder of your code, in the places where the array size is needed, the change takes care of itself. You simply change the value of the constant variable; then, every place it's used, the new value is automatically inserted.

Step 1: Start Your Compiler

Start your compiler if it is not already running.

Step 2: Open the Project 6-2 File

Open your **Proj6_2.java** file, and save it as **Proj6_3.java**.

Step 3: Modify Your Code

Modify your code so that it looks exactly like the code shown below.

```
// Proj6_3

// These are the classes needed for your applet to execute properly.
import java.awt.*;
import java.applet.*;
import java.awt.event.*;

// This is your class definition.
public class Proj6_3 extends Applet implements ActionListener
{
    // One label will be used to prompt the user.
    // One text field will be used for user input.
    // The ints are for an array, a subscript, and a value holder.
    Label lblResponse1;
```

```
    TextField txtResponse;
    int element, value;
    int simpleArray[];
    // This is the Java version of a constant variable.
    final int arraySize = 10;

    // This code executes when the applet initializes.
    public void init()
    {
        // This gives layout control to the programmer.
        setLayout(null);
        // The following lines allocate memory to the array
        // based on the "final" variable.
        simpleArray = new int[arraySize];
        element = 0;

        // The label and text field are being added.
        lblResponse1 = new Label("Enter 10 numbers:");
        lblResponse1.setBounds(30, 30, 250, 20);
        add(lblResponse1);

        txtResponse = new TextField(5);
        txtResponse.setBounds(300, 30, 50, 20);
        txtResponse.addActionListener(this);
        add(txtResponse);
    }

    // When the Enter key is pressed the value in the text field will
    // be assigned to the proper array element.
    public void actionPerformed(ActionEvent e)
    {
        if (element == 10)
            showStatus("This array only takes 10 numbers!");
        value = Integer.parseInt(txtResponse.getText());
        simpleArray[element] = value;
        element++;
        txtResponse.setText("");
        repaint();
    }

    public void paint (Graphics g)
    {
        // These are the position variables for g.drawstring.
        int xpos = 20, ypos = 80;

        // Everything else we need is included in the for loop.
        // Don't forget the braces for the body of code.
        for (int position = 0; position <= simpleArray.length;
position++){
            g.drawString ("Element # " + position + " holds the value "
+ simpleArray[position] +".", xpos, ypos);
            ypos += 15;
        }
    }
}
```

Step 4: Save Your Program

Once you have finished typing in your code, save it one final time before compiling the program.

Step 5: Compile and Run

Enter the commands necessary to compile and run your program. If errors occur during the compile, check your code, correct any errors, and rerun the program.

Your output should look exactly like the output from Project 6-2.

Step 6: Review Your Code

Explain what was accomplished by modifying the code.

1. Write down each line of code that was modified. Explain each modification.

_____

_____

_____

_____

_____

_____

_____

_____

_____

_____

When you're finished, discuss your answers with your teacher and classmates to reinforce your ability to analyze Java code.

PROJECT 6-4:
Compiling Survey Results Using Two Arrays (B)

In this project, you're going to use two arrays to compile and display survey results. This is an extremely useful application for arrays. You're giving the user control over inputting the results collected into one array; then, you accumulate the results into another array, and display the results to screen.

Step 1: Start Your Compiler

Start your compiler if it is not already running.

Step 2: Open the Project 6-3 File

Open your **Proj6_3.java** file, and save it as **Proj6_4.java**.

Step 3: Modify Your Code

Modify your code so that it looks exactly like the code shown below.

```
// Proj6_4

// These are the classes needed for your applet to execute properly.
import java.awt.*;
import java.applet.*;
import java.awt.event.*;

// This is your class definition.
public class Proj6_4 extends Applet implements ActionListener
{
    // Two labels will be used to prompt the user.
    // One text field will be used for user input.
    // The ints are subscripts and input values.
    Label lblResponse1, lblResponse2;
    TextField txtResponse;
    int element, value;
    // These are the arrays that will be used.
    int simpleArray[];
    int responseArray[];
    // These are the Java version of constant variables.
    final int arraySize = 20;
    final int responseSize = 4;

    // This code executes when the applet initializes.
    public void init()
    {
        // This gives layout control to the programmer.
        setLayout(null);
        // The following lines allocate memory to the arrays
        // based on the "final" variables and initialize the subscript.
        simpleArray = new int[arraySize];
        responseArray = new int[responseSize];
        element = 0;

        // The labels and text field are being added.
        lblResponse1 = new Label("Enter the participant's response:");
        lblResponse1.setBounds(30, 30, 250, 20);
        add(lblResponse1);

        lblResponse2 = new Label("1 - Agree, 2 - Disagree, 3 - No Opinion,
Zero to End");
        lblResponse2.setBounds(30, 45, 250, 20);
        add(lblResponse2);

        txtResponse = new TextField(5);
        txtResponse.setBounds(300, 30, 50, 20);
        txtResponse.addActionListener(this);
        add(txtResponse);

    }

    // When the Enter key is pressed the value in the text field will
```

```
        // be assigned to the proper array element in the simple array
        // and the response accumulator array.
        public void actionPerformed(ActionEvent e)
        {
                if (element == 20)
                        showStatus("This array only takes 20 responses!");
                value = Integer.parseInt(txtResponse.getText());
                simpleArray[element] = value;

                if (value == 1)
                        ++responseArray[value];

                else if (value == 2)
                        ++responseArray[value];

                else if (value == 3)
                        ++responseArray[value];

                element++;
                txtResponse.setText("");

                repaint();
        }

        public void paint (Graphics g)
        {
                // These are the position variables for g.drawstring.
                int xpos = 20, ypos = 80;

                // Everything else we need is included in the for loop.
                // The for loop will allow the program to display the
                // responses accumulated in the response array.
                for (int accumulator = 1; accumulator < responseArray.length;
accumulator++){
                        g.drawString ("Response choice " + accumulator + " recorded
" + responseArray[accumulator] + " responses.", xpos, ypos);
                        ypos += 15;
                }
        }
}
```

Step 4: Save Your Program

Once you have finished typing in your code, save it one final time before compiling the program.

Step 5: Compile and Run

Enter the commands necessary to compile and run your program. If errors occur during the compile, check your code, correct any errors, and rerun the program.

Your output should look like the following:

```
Response choice 1 recorded "X" responses.

Response choice 2 recorded "X" responses.

Response choice 3 recorded "X" responses.
```

The "X" will be replaced by the actual number of responses entered by the user. You will also notice that the accumulators change as the user enters the responses.

Step 6: Review Your Code

Explain what was accomplished by modifying the code.

1. Explain the following block of code:

```
        // The labels and text field are being added.
        lblResponse1 = new Label("Enter the participant's response:");
        lblResponse1.setBounds(30, 30, 250, 20);
        add(lblResponse1);

        lblResponse2 = new Label("1 - Agree, 2 - Disagree, 3 - No Opinion,
Zero to End");
        lblResponse2.setBounds(30, 45, 250, 20);
        add(lblResponse2);

        txtResponse = new TextField(5);
        txtResponse.setBounds(300, 30, 50, 20);
        txtResponse.addActionListener(this);
        add(txtResponse);
```

_____

_____

_____

_____

_____

_____

_____

_____

_____

2. Explain the following block of code:

```
public void actionPerformed(ActionEvent e)
{
        if (element == 20)
                showStatus("This array only takes 20 responses!");
        value = Integer.parseInt(txtResponse.getText());
        simpleArray[element] = value;

        if (value == 1)
                ++responseArray[value];

        else if (value == 2)
                ++responseArray[value];

        else if (value == 3)
```

```
            ++responseArray[value];

        element++;
        txtResponse.setText("");

        repaint();
}
```

_____
_____
_____
_____
_____
_____
_____
_____
_____
_____

3. Explain the potential problems that would occur if you were to use for loops here as you might in C++.

_____
_____
_____
_____
_____

4. Explain each of the declared items shown in the code below. Identify what they are, their type, and any values assigned to them.

```
Label lblResponse1, lblResponse2;
TextField txtResponse;
int element, value;

int simpleArray[];
int responseArray[];

final int arraySize = 20;
final int responseSize = 4;
```

_____
_____
_____
_____
_____

138

_____
_____
_____
_____

5. What purpose do each of the items in Question 4 serve in your program?

_____
_____
_____
_____
_____
_____
_____
_____
_____
_____

6. Explain the following block of code:

```
public void paint (Graphics g)
{

        int xpos = 20, ypos = 80;

        for (int accumulator = 1; accumulator < responseArray.length;
accumulator++){
                g.drawString ("Response choice " + accumulator + " recorded
" + responseArray[accumulator] + " responses.", xpos, ypos);
                ypos += 15;
        }
}
```

_____
_____
_____
_____
_____
_____
_____
_____
_____

When you're finished, discuss your answers with your teacher and classmates to reinforce your ability to analyze Java code.

You're well on your way to mastering arrays!

Another important need of programmers and users is to be able to sort data. Collecting the data and storing it is only part of the solution. You need to be able to put the data in a logical, practical order. The **bubble sort** is an easy solution to sorting. Although it will run slowly when used with large arrays, it will serve our needs for the time being. The reason this type of sort is called a bubble sort is that with each pass through the sorting loop, the smaller numbers "bubble" their way to the top.

Sorting is attracting some of the most intensive research in data processing today. That's because almost every institution has data it needs to sort.

Step 1: Start Your Compiler

Start your compiler if it is not already running.

Step 2: Open the Project 6-3 File

Open your **Proj6_3.java** file, and save it as **Proj6_5.java**.

Step 3: Modify Your Code

Modify your code so that it looks exactly like the code shown below.

```
// Proj6_5

// These are the classes needed for your applet to execute properly.
import java.awt.*;
import java.applet.*;
import java.awt.event.*;

// This is your class definition.
public class Proj6_5 extends Applet implements ActionListener
{
    // One label will be used to prompt the user.
    // One text field will be used for user input.
    // The ints are for an array, a subscript, a value holder, and
    // for the swap variable.
    Label lblResponse1;
    TextField txtResponse;
    Button sortButton;
    int element, value;
    int swap, loops;
    int simpleArray[];
    // This is the Java version of a constant variable.
    final int arraySize = 10;

    // This code executes when the applet initializes.
    public void init()
    {
        // This gives layout control to the programmer.
        setLayout(null);
        // The following lines allocate memory to the array
```

```
                // based on the "final" variable.
                simpleArray = new int[arraySize];
                element = 0;

                // The label and text field are being added.
                lblResponse1 = new Label("Enter 10 numbers:");
                lblResponse1.setBounds(30, 30, 250, 20);
                add(lblResponse1);

                txtResponse = new TextField(5);
                txtResponse.setBounds(300, 30, 50, 20);
                txtResponse.addActionListener(this);
                add(txtResponse);

                // This button will cause the bubble sort to execute.
                sortButton = new Button("Sort Array");
                sortButton.setBounds(400, 30, 150, 20);
                add(sortButton);
                sortButton.addActionListener(this);
        }

        // When the Enter key is pressed the value in the text field will
        // be assigned to the proper array element.
        public void actionPerformed(ActionEvent e)
        {
                // This is the code to be performed if the user presses
                // the Enter key - it's based on the text field.
                if (e.getSource() == txtResponse)
                {
                        if (element == 10)
                                showStatus("This array only takes 10 numbers!");
                        value = Integer.parseInt(txtResponse.getText());
                        simpleArray[element] = value;
                        element++;
                        txtResponse.setText("");
                        repaint();
                }

                // This is the bubble sort and it's executed when the user clicks
                // the button.
                if (e.getSource() == sortButton)
                {
                        for (loops = 0; loops < arraySize -1 ; loops++){

                                for(element = 0; element < arraySize - 1; element++)
                                {
                                        if (simpleArray[element] > simpleArray[element
+ 1])
                                        {
                                                swap = simpleArray[element];
                                                simpleArray[element] =
simpleArray[element + 1];

                                                simpleArray[element + 1] = swap;
                                        }
                                }
```

141

```
                }
                repaint();
        }
    }

    public void paint (Graphics g)
    {
            // These are the position variables for g.drawstring.
            int xpos = 30, ypos = 120;

            // The for loop displays the elements in the array.
            // Don't forget the braces for the body of code.
            g.drawString("These are the positions of the array contents.", 30,
90);
            for (int position = 0; position <= simpleArray.length;
position++){
                    g.drawString ("Element # " + position + " holds the value "
+ simpleArray[position] +".", xpos, ypos);
                    ypos += 15;
            }
    }
}
```

Step 4: Save Your Program

Once you have finished typing in your code, save it one final time before compiling the program.

Step 5: Compile and Run

Enter the commands necessary to compile and run your program. If errors occur during the compile, check your code, correct any errors, and rerun the program.

The first part of your output should look exactly like the output from Project 6-3. Once you click the **Sort Array** button, there will be one noticeable difference—the values should be in *ascending* order.

Step 6: Review Your Code

Explain what was accomplished by modifying the code.

1. Write down the items from the block below that have been modified from Project 6-3 or are new to this project. Explain the purpose of the modifications or additions.

```
Label lblResponse1;
TextField txtResponse;
Button sortButton;
int element, value;
int swap, loops;
int simpleArray[];
// This is the Java version of a constant variable.
final int arraySize = 10;
```

_____

_____

_____

_____

_____

_____

_____

_____

_____

2. The following block of code is your entire bubble sort. Explain why two for statements are used.

```
        if (e.getSource() == sortButton)
        {
            for (loops = 0; loops < arraySize -1 ; loops++){

                for(element = 0; element < arraySize - 1; element++)
                {
                    if (simpleArray[element] > simpleArray[element
+ 1])
                    {
                        swap = simpleArray[element];
                        simpleArray[element] =
simpleArray[element + 1];

                        simpleArray[element + 1] = swap;
                    }
                }
            }
            repaint();
        }
```

_____

_____

_____

_____

_____

_____

_____

_____

_____

3. Explain the body of the nested for statement.

_____

_____

_____

_____

4. Explain the swap variable.

_____

_____

_____

_____

_____

5. Explain the loops variable.

_____

_____

_____

_____

_____

When you're finished, discuss your answers with your teacher and classmates to reinforce your ability to analyze Java code.

Now you are capable of coding bubble sorts!

PROJECT 6-6 : Searching

(B)

Another important need of programmers and users is to be able to find data. In this project, you will learn how to perform a simple _linear search_. This type of search works well with small and un-sorted arrays. However, for large arrays, linear searching is inefficient; for these we will need to develop a _binary search_ method.

Step 1: Start Your Compiler

Start your compiler if it is not already running.

Step 2: Open the Project 6-4 File

Open your **Proj6_4.java** file, and save it as **Proj6_6.java**.

Step 3: Modify Your Code

Modify your code so that it looks exactly like the code shown below.

```
// Proj6_6

// These are the classes needed for your applet to execute properly.
import java.awt.*;
import java.applet.*;
import java.awt.event.*;

// This is your class definition.
public class Proj6_6 extends Applet implements ActionListener
```

```
{
    // One label will be used to prompt the user for array values,
    // the other will prompt for the search value.
    // The text fields will be used for user input.
    // The ints are for an array, a subscript, a value holder, the search
value
    // and for the found test.
    Label lblResponse1, lblSearcher;
    TextField txtResponse, txtSearcher;
    Button sortButton;
    int element, value, searcher;
    int foundElement;
    int simpleArray[];
    // This is the Java version of a constant variable.
    final int arraySize = 10;

    // This code executes when the applet initializes.
    public void init()
    {
            // This gives layout control to the programmer.
            setLayout(null);
            // The following lines allocate memory to the array
            // based on the "final" variable.
            simpleArray = new int[arraySize];
            element = 0;

            // The labels and text fields are being added.
            lblResponse1 = new Label("Enter 10 numbers:");
            lblResponse1.setBounds(30, 30, 250, 20);
            add(lblResponse1);

            txtResponse = new TextField(5);
            txtResponse.setBounds(300, 30, 50, 20);
            txtResponse.addActionListener(this);
            add(txtResponse);

            lblSearcher = new Label("Enter the number you want to find:");
            lblSearcher.setBounds(30, 60, 250, 20);
            add(lblSearcher);

            txtSearcher = new TextField(5);
            txtSearcher.setBounds(300, 60, 50, 20);
            txtSearcher.addActionListener(this);
            add(txtSearcher);
    }

    // When the Enter key is pressed the value in the text field will
    // be assigned to the proper array element.
    public void actionPerformed(ActionEvent e)
    {
            // This is the code to be performed if the user presses
            // the Enter key - it's based on the text field.
            if (e.getSource() == txtResponse)
            {
                    if (element == 10)
```

145

```
                    showStatus("This array only takes 10 numbers!");
                value = Integer.parseInt(txtResponse.getText());
                simpleArray[element] = value;
                element++;
                txtResponse.setText("");
                repaint();
        }

        // This is the linear search and it's executed when the user
        // enters a value in the search text field and then presses Enter.
        if (e.getSource() == txtSearcher)
        {
                int found = -1;
                searcher = Integer.parseInt(txtSearcher.getText());
                for(element = 0; element < arraySize; element++)
                {
                        if (simpleArray[element] == searcher)
                        {
                                found = simpleArray[element];
                                foundElement = element;
                                break;
                        }
                }

                // These lines display the search results in the status
window.
                if (found != -1)
                        showStatus("The number you are seeking " + searcher +
" is in element " + foundElement + ".");
                else
                        showStatus("The number you are seeking " + searcher +
" was not found.");
        }
    }

    public void paint (Graphics g)
    {
        // These are the position variables for g.drawstring.
        int xpos = 30, ypos = 120;

        // The for loop displays the elements in the array.
        // Don't forget the braces for the body of code.
        g.drawString("These are the array contents.", 30, 100);
        for (int position = 0; position <= simpleArray.length;
position++){
                g.drawString ("Element # " + position + " holds the value "
+ simpleArray[position] +".", xpos, ypos);
                ypos += 15;
        }
    }
}
```

Step 4: Save Your Program

Once you have finished typing in your code, save it one final time before compiling the program.

Step 5: Compile and Run

Enter the commands necessary to compile and run your program. If errors occur during the compile, check your code, correct any errors, and rerun the program.

The input should look exactly like that from Project 6-3. The second part should return the value for which you searched, or you will be notified if the value was *not* found.

Step 6: Review Your Code

Explain what was accomplished by modifying the code:

1. Explain the following line of code:

```
if (e.getSource() == txtSearcher)
```

_____

_____

_____

2. The block of code below is the entire linear search. Explain this block of code.

```
if (e.getSource() == txtSearcher)
{
    int found = -1;
    searcher = Integer.parseInt(txtSearcher.getText());
    for(element = 0; element < arraySize; element++)
    {
        if (simpleArray[element] == searcher)
        {
            found = simpleArray[element];
            foundElement = element;
            break;
        }
    }
}
```

_____

_____

_____

_____

_____

_____

_____

_____

_____

3. Explain the block of code below.

```
            if (found != -1)
                    showStatus("The number you are seeking " + searcher +
" is in element " + foundElement + ".");
            else
                    showStatus("The number you are seeking " + searcher +
" was not found.");
        }
```

_____

_____

_____

_____

4. Explain why you "break" out of the search loop.

_____

_____

_____

_____

When you're finished, discuss your answers with your teacher and classmates to reinforce your ability to analyze Java code.

Now you are capable of coding linear searches.

Summary

This lesson was an overview of a number of useful data manipulation tools. You learned how to create an array, and how to create output so that it's easy to read and interpret.

Initializing the array is very important. We discussed the fact that the user may need to input the data to be manipulated. Then you allowed the user to input the data collected for your program. You also discovered that the size of the array needs to be set before the array is compiled. The reason for this is that the compiler sets aside a specific amount of memory for the array. By using a constant variable, you were able to add scalability to your program. In other words, if the array ever needed to change size, all you would need to modify is the value of the constant variable. You then learned about manipulation. The first pure manipulation you performed was a bubble sort. Bubble sorts are an easy way to put data in either ascending or descending order. You learned how important it is for a user to be able to access data, often in a specific order. Banks, for instance, put checks from your checking account into ascending order. Direct mail organizations sort their outgoing mailings by ZIP code in order to get reduced postage rates. So, you can see the importance of sorting.

Finally, you performed a simple linear search. You learned that linear searches are useful in small, unsorted arrays. Binary searching is more practical for larger arrays.

LESSON 6 REVIEW QUESTIONS

SHORT ANSWER

Define the following in the space provided.

1. Arrays

2. Subscript

3. Explicitly

4. Implicitly

5. Element

6. Constant variable

7. Final

8. Linear search

9. Binary search

_____

_____

_____

10. Off-by-one error

_____

_____

_____

11. Logical and operator (&&)

_____

_____

_____

12. Bubble sort

_____

_____

_____

13. Sort

_____

_____

_____

14. Ascending

_____

_____

_____

15. Descending

_____

_____

_____

16. Scalability

_____

_____

_____

17. Status window

_____

_____

_____

18. Graphic object

_____

_____

_____

WRITTEN QUESTIONS

Write your answers to the following questions in the space provided.

1. Explain off-by-one errors.

_____

_____

_____

_____

_____

2. Explain the benefit of using a constant variable (final) to set the size of an array.

_____

_____

_____

3. Explain why the number of the first element in an array is zero.

_____

_____

_____

4. Explain the difference between painting and using the status window.

_____

_____

_____

5. Explain the difference between a linear search and a binary search.

_____

_____

_____

_____

_____

_____

_____

6. Explain sorting.

_____

_____

_____

7. Explain how a bubble sort works.

_____

_____

_____

8. Explain the purpose of using the swap variable in the bubble sort in Project 6-5.

_____

_____

_____

TESTING YOUR SKILLS

Estimated Time:

Application 6-1 30 minutes
Application 6-2 2 hours

APPLICATION 6-1

Using your **Proj6_5.java** file, modify the code to create a descending order bubble sort. Save your file as **App6_1.java**.

APPLICATION 6-2

Create three separate buttons/calculations for your **Project 6-4** survey results program. In your original program you allowed the user to enter survey results; then your program displayed the compiled results by answer. Now, add three separate calculations: calculate and display the mean (average), the median (the middle number), and the mode (the answer that appears the most often). Use **Proj6_4.java** as the basis for this application. Save your file as **App6_2.java**.

CRITICAL THINKING (A)

Estimated Time: 2 hours each

ACTIVITY 6-1

Create an array that accumulates, and then displays, the result of a random number generator that mimics the repetitive tossing of dice.

ACTIVITY 6-2

Create a binary search routine to use on a large, sorted array. Create a large array of at least 100 elements, populate the array with any method you choose, and then perform a binary search.

APPLICATIONS

On completion of this lesson, you should be able to:

- Define Java applications.
- Explain the differences between applets and applications.
- Design the layout for Java applications.
- Integrate control structures into applications.
- Produce working applications from the instructions provided.

⏱ **Estimated Time: 6 ½ hours**

Introduction

The basic difference between Java *applets* and Java *applications* is that the applications are stand-alone. Applications do not require the applet viewer or a Web browser to execute. When Java was first introduced, its major claim to fame was the bells and whistles it enabled you to add to Web pages, such as animated text and graphics. Over the past few years, Java has evolved into a software application development tool. Sometimes defined as C++ done right, Java is now being used to develop applications such as Web servers, network operating systems, and database server engines.

In this lesson, you will be introduced to the basics of Java applications. If you have programmed in C++, you will probably notice that Java applications have a closer resemblance to this "parent" language than Java applets do. First and foremost, you will recognize the C++ main function, or the main *method* as it is called in Java. The main method must have this first line:

```
public static void main (String args [])
```

If it does not, the Java interpreter will not be able to execute your program.

As in C++ programming, you will still be creating a class; however, it won't be instantiated in these projects. You will still be required to prompt the user for input, and you will be required to provide feedback to the user in the form of output. At this point, you will move away from the GUI and back into console applications. The main reason you will not be using GUI objects in your applications is that there are still various classes from different software vendors that make Java GUI components somewhat proprietary. In light of this, we will address applications from a non-GUI point of view. However, your teacher can point out the classes that can be used to make your applications GUI-oriented based on the specific compiler you are using.

This lesson will focus on the following:

■ **Defining Java applications and learning the differences between applets and applications.** You will be shown the differences between applets and applications, and these differences will be explained to strengthen your understanding of each program type.

■ **Designing the layout for Java applications.** You will begin designing simple Java applications that allow you to become familiar with the layout of these applications. Even though these applications are similar to applets, there are some differences.

■ **Integrating control structures in applications.** Since you are back to console applications, your code will now need to reflect control structures more so than was required in applets. The sequence control structure will now be integrated, and the selection and repetition structures will be used where needed.

■ **Producing working applications from the instructions provided.** As in every lesson in this book, you will code working applications. You will be converting existing applets into applications. *REMEMBER:* There is no better way to learn how to program than to program!

So, strap yourself in, get ready to work, and prepare to learn about Java applications!

P R O J E C T   7 - 1 : Miles-to-Kilometers Conversion

In Lesson 1, your applets were very simple. For example, in Project 1-1 you simply asked the user to input the number of miles run, and you coded a conversion to kilometers that provided them with the number of kilometers they had run.

Now, you will use the same program example to code your first Java application. You will modify Project 1-1 into a Java application.

Step 1: Start Your Compiler

If your compiler is not already running, start it now. If there is a New Project option included with your compiler, and you are able to choose a "Console Application," you may want to do so. Such an option is included with Microsoft J++ 6.0 and creates a default Java file layout that provides you with a starting point. However, it is not necessary.

Step 2: Type in Your Code

Type your code exactly as shown below. Save this program with the name **Proj7_1.java**. Remember to save your work often as you type.

```
// Proj7_1
import java.io.*;


public class Proj7_1
{
    public static void main (String[] args) throws IOException
    {
        int MI = 0;
```

154

```
        double KM = 0;

        System.out.print("Enter the number of miles you've run: ");
        MI = System.in.read();
        MI = MI - 48;
        KM = MI / .62;

        System.out.println("You have run " + KM + " kilometers.");
    }
}
```

Step 3: Review Your Code

To test your understanding of the program components, answer the following questions in the space provided.

1. Explain the `import java.io.*;` line.

_____

_____

_____

2. Explain `public class Proj_1 {`.

_____

_____

_____

3. Explain `public static void main (String[] args) throws IOException {`.

_____

_____

_____

4. What are the { } used for?

_____

_____

_____

5. What are KM and MI? What is the significance of `int`?

_____

_____

_____

6. Explain `System.out.print("Enter the number of miles you've run: ");`.

_____

_____

_____

7. Explain `MI = System.in.read();`.

_____

_____

_____

8. Explain the limitations of the `System.in.read()` method.

_____

_____

_____

9. Explain the following line of code: `MI = MI - 48;`. (***HINT:*** ASCII code).

_____

_____

_____

10. Explain `System.out.println("You have run " + KM + " kilometers.");`.

_____

_____

_____

11. Why are you not required to end the application with `return 0;`?

_____

_____

_____

Reviewing the correct answers to the above questions with your teacher and classmates will help you understand the basic components of a Java application. It's important to know exactly what is happening in your program so that you are able to correct any errors that occur.

Step 4: Compile and Run

Enter the commands necessary to compile and run your program. If errors occur during the compile, check your code, correct any errors, and rerun the program.

Remember to save your program any time you make changes!

Step 5: Review Your Output

Your output should look like the following:

```
Enter the number of miles you've run: 6
You have run 9.6774 kilometers.
```

Answer the following in the space provided.

1. What limitations are forced on the user by the `System.in.read()` method?

_____

_____

_____

156

2. Why does the application stop execution instead of waiting for user response?

_____

_____

_____

If you are not sure of the answers to the above questions—experiment! When you think you have it figured out, write down your answers in the space provided above. When you're finished, discuss your answers with your teacher and classmates to reinforce your ability to analyze Java code.

P R O J E C T 7 - 2 : Survey Results

This program will convert the applet you completed in Project 5-5. You will collect the same survey results, but in a somewhat different manner.

Once again you will be using a console application. You will prompt the user for input and will accumulate the survey results that they enter. You will notice that the application uses the built-in sequence structure and then takes advantage of both a repetition and a selection structure. Once the user inputs all the information, the program will display the compilation and then terminate.

Step 1: Start Your Compiler

If your compiler is not already running, start it now.

Step 2: Type in Your Code

Type in the code as shown below. Save the program as **Proj7_2.java**. Save your program regularly as you type the code.

 HOT TIP

More experienced programmers may want to make a copy of the *Proj5_5.java* file, rename it **Proj7_2.java**, and then modify the code where appropriate. Make sure your final code matches what's shown.

```
// Proj7_2

import java.io.*;

public class Proj7_2
{

    public static void main (String[] args) throws IOException
    {
            int response, Acount, Dcount, NOcount;
            Acount = Dcount = NOcount = 0;

            System.out.print("A - Agree; D - Disagree; N - No Opinion; X -
Exit\n");
            System.out.print("All responses must be in CAPS!\n\n");
            System.out.print("Enter survey response: ");
            response = System.in.read();

            while (response != 'X')
            {
```

```
                    switch(response)
                    {
                    case 'A':
                    case 'a':
                            ++Acount;
                            break;

                    case 'D':
                    case 'd':
                            ++Dcount;
                            break;

                    case 'N':
                    case 'n':
                            ++NOcount;
                            break;

                    default:
                            System.out.print("Enter a correct response!");
                            break;
                    }

                    System.in.skip(2);
                    System.out.print("Enter survey response: ");
                    response = System.in.read();
            }
        System.out.print(Acount + " agree, " + Dcount + " disagree, " + "
and " + NOcount + " have no opinion.");
    }
}
```

Answer the following questions regarding the above code:

1. Explain what each of the `System.out.print` commands does at the beginning of the main method.

_____

_____

_____

_____

_____

_____

2. Explain, in general, what the \n escape character does.

_____

_____

_____

3. Explain the following line of code:

```
response = System.in.read();
```

_____

_____

_____

4. Explain the following line of code:

```
while (response != 'X')
```

_____

_____

_____

5. Explain the following line of code:

```
System.in.skip(2);
```

_____

_____

_____

6. Explain the following block of code:

```
switch(response)
{
case 'A':
case 'a':
     ++Acount;
     break;
```

_____

_____

_____

7. Explain the following block of code:

```
default:
     System.out.print("Enter a correct response!");
     break;
```

_____

_____

_____

Step 3: Save Your Program

When you have finished typing the code, save your program once more before moving on to the next step.

Step 4: Compile and Run

Enter the commands necessary to compile and run your program. If errors occur during the compile, check your code, correct any errors, and rerun the program.

Remember to save your program any time you make changes!

If you have typed the code correctly, you should now have an application interface that looks something like the following:

```
A - Agree; D- Disagree; N - No Opinion; X - Exit
All responses must be in CAPS!

Enter survey response:
```

Congratulations! You have now programmed an application that uses the built-in sequence structure as well as a repetition and selection structure.

PROJECT 7-3 : Survey Results with Two Arrays

In this lesson you will convert the code from Project 6-4 into a Java application. You will again use the method main, along with two arrays and two final variables as subscripts. However, you will be able to use two for loops to populate both arrays, instead of the if structures originally used.

You will also implement an additional "escape character," the \t. The \t instructs the text on an output line to "jump over" one tab stop. You will see how the \t actually helps format the output from your program.

Step 1: Start Your Compiler

If your compiler is not already running, start it now.

Step 2: Type in Your Code

Type in the code as shown below. Save the program as **Proj7_3.java**. *REMEMBER:* Save often as you type in the code.

```
// Proj7_3

import java.io.*;

public class Proj7_3
{

    public static void main (String[] args) throws IOException
    {
        int element = 0;
        int value = 0;
```

```
        final int arraySize = 20;
        final int responseSize = 4;
        int simpleArray[];
        int responseArray[] = {0};

        simpleArray = new int[arraySize];
        responseArray = new int[responseSize];

        System.out.print("\nEnter A - Agree, D - Disagree, N - No
Opinion\n");
        System.out.print("This array will only take 20 entries!\n\n");
        System.out.print("Please enter your survey results.\n");

        for (element = 0; element < arraySize; element++)
        {
            System.out.print("\nEnter a result: ");
            value = System.in.read();
            simpleArray[element] = value;
            System.in.skip(2);
        }

        for (element = 0; element < arraySize; element++)
        {
            if (simpleArray[element] == 'A')
            {
                value = 1;
                ++responseArray[value];
            }
            else if (simpleArray[element] == 'D')
            {
                value = 2;
                ++responseArray[value];
            }
            else if (simpleArray[element] == 'N')
            {
                value = 3;
                ++responseArray[value];
            }
        }

        System.out.print("Response\t\t" + "Number of\n");

        for (value = 1; value < responseSize; value++)
            System.out.print("\t" + value + "\t\t" +
responseArray[value] + "\n");
    }
}
```

Step 3: Save Your Program

When you have finished typing the code, save your program once more before moving on to the next step.

Step 4: Compile and Run

Enter the commands necessary to compile and run your program. If errors occur during the compile, check your code, correct any errors, and rerun the program.

Remember to save your program any time you make changes!

Your output should look like the following:

```
Enter A - Agree, D - Disagree, N - No Opinion
This array will only take 20 entries!

Please enter your survey results.

Enter a result:
(This will repeat 20 times. At the conclusion the following will appear:)
Response                              Number of
      1                                   7
      2                                   7
      3                                   6
```

You need to be aware of a few things regarding this program: Error-checking is *not* being performed; therefore, you can enter anything as a response and it will be accepted. If you press the Enter key without entering a value, the program will continue to execute as if you did enter a value. Invalid responses are simply not accumulated.

Step 5: Explain Your Program

Explain each line or block of code in the program in the space provided.

```
// Proj7_3

import java.io.*;

public class Proj7_3
{
```

_____

_____

_____

```
public static void main (String[] args) throws IOException
{
```

_____

_____

```
int element = 0;
int value = 0;
final int arraySize = 20;
final int responseSize = 4;
int simpleArray[];
int responseArray[] = {0};
```

```
simpleArray = new int[arraySize];
responseArray = new int[responseSize];
```

```
        System.out.print("\nEnter A - Agree, D - Disagree, N - No
Opinion\n");
        System.out.print("This array will only take 20 entries!\n\n");
        System.out.print("Please enter your survey results.\n");
```

```
for (element = 0; element < arraySize; element++)
{
     System.out.print("\nEnter a result: ");
     value = System.in.read();
     simpleArray[element] = value;
     System.in.skip(2);
}
```

```
for (element = 0; element < arraySize; element++)
{
     if (simpleArray[element] == 'A')
     {
          value = 1;
```

```
                    ++responseArray[value];
            }
            else if (simpleArray[element] == 'D')
            {
                    value = 2;
                    ++responseArray[value];
            }
            else if (simpleArray[element] == 'N')
            {
                    value = 3;
                    ++responseArray[value];
            }
    }
```

_____

_____

_____

_____

_____

_____

```
        System.out.print("Response\t\t" + "Number of\n");

        for (value = 1; value < responseSize; value++)
                System.out.print("\t" + value + "\t\t" +
responseArray[value] + "\n");
    }
```

_____

_____

_____

_____

_____

Summary

This lesson showed you how to convert applets into applications. You were first introduced to what actually constitutes a Java application. A Java application is a standalone program, whereas an applet requires an applet viewer or a Web browser. A Java application also requires a main method, the Java version of the C++ main function. Without this, the Java interpreter will not be able to execute your program.

In Java applications, you still create a class as you do in C++ programming; however, the class is not instantiated. You still prompted the user for input, and you provided feedback to the user in the form of output. The most noticeable difference between applets and the applications you wrote was the absence of a GUI. In this lesson you wrote console applications. The main reason for this is that there are still various classes from different software vendors that make Java GUI components somewhat proprietary.

You now have the ability to convert any of your applets into applications. And you can even create much longer applications from scratch, similar to those in C++, for whatever need you might come across. Java gives you the best of both worlds!

LESSON 7 REVIEW QUESTIONS

SHORT ANSWER

Define the following in the space provided.

1. Application

2. Applet

3. Applet viewer

4. Control structures

5. GUI

6. Web browser

_____

_____

_____

7. Main method

_____

_____

_____

8. Java interpreter

_____

_____

_____

9. Escape characters

_____

_____

_____

10. Backslash

_____

_____

_____

11. Console application

_____

_____

_____

12. Sequence structure

_____

_____

_____

13. Repetition structure

_____

_____

_____

14. Selection structure

_____

_____

_____

WRITTEN QUESTIONS

Write your answers to the following questions in the space provided.

1. Explain the following line of code:

```
public static void main(String args []).
```

_____

_____

_____

2. Explain why the main method throws exceptions.

_____

_____

_____

3. Write the section of code that should be added to the code in Question 1 regarding exceptions.

_____

_____

_____

4. Explain the following line of code:

```
value = System.in.read();
```

_____

_____

_____

5. Explain the following line of code:

```
System.in.skip(2);
```

_____

_____

_____

6. Explain the following line of code:

```
System.out.print();
```

_____

_____

_____

7. Research and list the various escape characters. Explain what each escape character does.

_____

_____

_____

_____

_____

_____

_____

_____

8. Explain the following line of code:

```
import java.io.*;
```

_____

_____

_____

_____

_____

CRITICAL THINKING

 **Estimated Time: 6–8 hours**

(The Testing Your Skills and Critical Thinking exercises for this lesson are being combined in order to give you more flexibility in practicing how to create Java applications.)

Choose three applets from any of the previous lessons (excluding the ones converted in this lesson's projects) and convert them into Java applications.

User-Defined Classes— Object-Oriented Programming

Introduction

In your use of classes in Java programming, you have been exposed to object-oriented programming. Everything in Java, with the exception of the primitive data types, is an object. Everything you have done in Java programming (at least in this project book) has made use of existing classes. We'll begin this lesson with a more in-depth discussion of classes.

Structures, the C *aggregate data type*, make the evolution to classes easy. If you have programmed in C/C++ you will remember that structures are basically collections of data types. They are a user-created type that do not need to consist of the same data type.

A class is also a user-created, *user-defined type*. However, a class contains methods as well as data. The data is referred to as *instance variables*, and the member functions are now referred to as *methods*. So now you have data, and things you can do with the data, all stored in the same place. The class is now referred to as an *object*, and it forms *the* unit of programming in Java and C++. This is the basis of *object-oriented programming*. Think about the implications—data and related methods that form a complete unit. The user can define classes, like structures. You create the data types that they need to work with. Plus, there are multitudes of classes available from various sources that you can also expand on or modify. As you will see, Java is quite an explosive language!

You will notice an important change in naming conventions in this lesson. You will be instructed to assign *meaningful* names instead of the "ProjX_X" used up to this point. It is important to use meaningful filenames to emphasize the relationship between classes. So, pay careful attention to the names used throughout this lesson.

You will also see that you can protect data from the user by limiting access to it. This is known as separating the *interface* from the *implementation*. In simpler terms, this means that the user can execute the program (the interface) without knowing the details of how it actually runs (the implementation). And isn't this the way all the programs you use work?

This lesson will focus on the following:

■ **Designing and defining a class.** You will start by using a simple class similar to others that you have created in this book, and then you will explore other class topics.

■ **Creating classes and class members.** Since you define the class, you will decide what the class will look like, what it will include, and what it will do. You'll begin to understand the proper way to keep data away from the user.

■ **Separating interface from implementation.** One of the major advantages of classes is that they provide you with a mechanism for protecting code from the user. You, as the programmer, decide how the user will gain access to the data. This is known as separating the interface (how the user uses the program) from the implementation (how the program works "under the hood").

■ **Accessing class members and controlling access to class members.** If you are going to separate interface from implementation, you need to provide users with a way to manipulate the data. These methods will also control what can be done with the data.

■ **Deriving a class.** Classes can be reused. After all, that's the beauty of object-oriented programming. Users can start with an existing class and *inherit* the set of properties into a new class. This is known as *inheritance*. You start with a *superclass* and *derive* a new class from an old one, while retaining the properties of the old one. Why reinvent the wheel?

PROJECT 8-1 : A Simple Class

In this project, you will be creating a class that will create a pet—your pet. You will be provided with the information needed to define the class. The emphasis will be on instance variables and the public methods that interface with them. You will be using this class throughout the lesson.

Step 1: Start Your Compiler

Start your compiler if it is not already running.

Step 2: Design Your Class

You will be creating a Pet class. It could be any pet, so when you create your pet think of the attributes that your pet may have.

1. Create your Pet class definition by writing it first in the space below. Your class will be called **Pet**. Your data members will be attributes that your Pet possesses, such as weight, color, breed, sounds, and so on. You also need to create methods. What does your pet do? You will not need to create the methods right away, but you should be able to define your data types.

    _____

    _____

    _____

_____

_____

_____

_____

2. In the space below, create a flowchart, narrative, or other explanation of how your methods will work alone and then together. For example, your dog may "speak" when asked, and will possibly tell you about itself when asked. You will need at least one of these two functions. Plus, you may need additional functions.

_____

_____

_____

_____

_____

_____

_____

_____

_____

_____

_____

_____

_____

3. Using the information from Step 2, lay out your method(s) in the space below.

_____

_____

_____

_____

_____

_____

_____

_____

_____

_____

_____

_____

_____

4. At this point you should have your class definition ready to go. You should have your instance variables and all of your methods. Did you remember to create a constructor that will initialize all your data variables to a consistent state? Remember, you should create at least one default constructor to initialize data members. If you have not created one, create your constructor on the lines below.

_____

_____

_____

Make sure that your instance variables are labeled as private and that your methods are labeled as public. This will help protect data from being accessed directly by users.

5. Lay out your applet in the space below. Insert comments in the appropriate places.

_____

_____

_____

_____

_____

_____

_____

_____

_____

_____

6. Organize your blocks of code in the space below.

_____

_____

_____

_____

_____

_____

_____

_____

_____

_____

_____

Step 3: Type in Your Code

Type your code in as you've written it above. Save the file as **Pet.java**.

Step 4: Save Your Program

Once you have finished typing in your code, save your code one final time before compiling your program.

Step 5: Compile and Run

Enter the commands necessary to compile and run your program. If errors occur during the compile, check your code, correct any errors, and rerun the program.

Your program should perform the tasks you listed in Step 1. If your program performs those tasks, it works properly.

Step 6: Review Your Code

Now that your program has run successfully, answer the following questions. Review your answers with your classmates and teacher.

1. How many class files did you need to import for your program to compile properly? List the class files you needed to use.

_____

_____

_____

_____

_____

_____

_____

_____

2. Explain the instance variables used to "define" your dog.

_____

_____

_____

_____

_____

_____

_____

_____

3. Explain each of your methods.

_____

_____

_____

_____

_____

_____

_____

4. Explain each of the GUI components used in your applet.

_____

_____

_____

_____

_____

_____

5. Explain the method used to gather input from the user.

_____

_____

_____

_____

_____

_____

6. Explain the method used to display the information about your pet.

_____

_____

_____

_____

_____

_____

Step 7: Check Your Code

The code below is just one example of creating a "dog." If your code is different and it works—that's great! Not everyone programs the same.

```
// Proj8_1

// These are the classes needed for this applet to execute.
import java.awt.*;
import java.awt.event.*;
import java.applet.Applet;


public class Pet extends Applet implements ActionListener
{
    // These are the private instance variables.
    private int weight;
    private String breed, color, sound;

    // These are the GUI components used for user input.
    Label lblIntro, lblWeight, lblBreed, lblColor, lblSound;
    TextField txtWeight, txtBreed, txtColor, txtSound;

    // The init method is performed when the applet initializes.
    public void init()
    {
        // The programmer has control over the layout.
        setLayout(null);

        lblIntro = new Label("DESCRIBE YOUR PET!");
        lblIntro.setBounds(90, 30, 150, 20);
        add(lblIntro);

        lblWeight = new Label("Enter the weight:");
        lblWeight.setBounds(30, 70, 125, 20);
        txtWeight = new TextField(10);
        txtWeight.setBounds(170, 70, 100, 20);
        add(lblWeight);
        add(txtWeight);

        lblBreed = new Label("Enter the breed:");
        lblBreed.setBounds(30, 100, 125, 20);
        txtBreed = new TextField(10);
        txtBreed.setBounds(170, 100, 100, 20);
        add(lblBreed);
        add(txtBreed);

        lblColor = new Label("Enter the color:");
        lblColor.setBounds(30, 130, 125, 20);
        txtColor = new TextField(10);
        txtColor.setBounds(170, 130, 100, 20);
        add(lblColor);
        add(txtColor);
```

```
        lblSound = new Label("Enter the sound it makes:");
        lblSound.setBounds(30, 160, 125, 20);
        txtSound = new TextField(10);
        txtSound.setBounds(170, 160, 100, 20);
        add(lblSound);
        add(txtSound);
        txtSound.addActionListener(this);
    }


    // When the Enter key is pressed the data is transferred from the GUI
    // to the instance variables.
    public void actionPerformed(ActionEvent e)
    {
        weight = Integer.parseInt(txtWeight.getText());
        breed = txtBreed.getText();
        color = txtColor.getText();
        sound = txtSound.getText();
        repaint();
    }


    // The paint method displays the output.
    public void paint (Graphics g)
    {
        g.drawString("The pet's weight is " + weight + ".", 30, 250);
        g.drawString("The pet's breed is " + breed + ".", 30, 280);
        g.drawString("The pet's color is " + color + ".", 30, 310);
        g.drawString("The pet makes this sound: " + sound + ".", 30, 340);
    }

}
```

Now you have a pet that you can change without a great deal of effort, and you don't need to clean up after it either!

PROJECT 8-2:
Separating Interface and Implementation

In this project, you will "enhance" your pet. Since we will be introducing a new concept in this project, we will provide the code for you to input. It will be your responsibility to research the code and explain what it does.

As you have learned, the purpose of a constructor is to initialize your private data members. In this project, you will use a constructor to call a method that receives input from the user. By doing this, you will be assigning data to private instance variables after the user inputs the information needed. This method will allow you to "pass" information from public variables to private variables using *encapsulation*.

The overall execution of this program will not look any different from the program in Project 8-1; however, the implementation will consist of two classes. One of the class definitions will be your PetClass, the other the interface called PetTest. PetTest will prompt the user for input and will pass the input on to the hidden instance variables in PetClass.

Feel free to enhance your dog beyond what's shown in the instruction.

Step 1: Start Your Compiler

Start your compiler if it is not already running.

Step 2: Type in Your Code

Type in your code for the PetClass file as follows. Save the file as **PetClass.java**.

```
// Proj8_2 PetClass Class Definition

public class PetClass
{
    private int weight;
    private String breed, color, sound;

    public PetClass()
    {
        setPet();
    }

    public void setPet ()
    {
        weight = 0;
        breed = "";
        color = "";
        sound = "";
    }

    public void setPet(int w, String b, String c, String s)
    {
        weight = w;
        breed = b;
        color = c;
        sound = s;
    }

    public int getWeight()
    {
        return weight;
    }

    public String getBreed()
    {
        return breed;
    }

    public String getColor()
```

```
        {
            return color;
        }

    public String getSound()
        {
            return sound;
        }
}
```

This file is your pet definition. It contains the instance variables and all the public methods needed to interface with the variables. At this point, this file does not even need to be compiled. It simply needs to sit in the same project folder as your other file, PetTest. **Import** statements do not need to be used if the class files(s) referred to in your program "live" in the same project folder as your main applet.

Now you need to type in your PetTest applet, which will provide the interface for your PetClass. Save this file as **PetTest.java**.

```
// Proj8_2
// The User Interface - PetTest.java

import java.awt.*;
import java.awt.event.*;
import java.applet.Applet;


public class PetTest extends Applet implements ActionListener
{
    private PetClass Pet;

    int w;
    String b, c, s;
    Label lblIntro, lblWeight, lblBreed, lblColor, lblSound;
    TextField txtWeight, txtBreed, txtColor, txtSound;

    public void init()
    {
            Pet = new PetClass();

            setLayout(null);

            lblIntro = new Label("DESCRIBE YOUR PET!");
            lblIntro.setBounds(90, 30, 150, 20);
            add(lblIntro);

            lblWeight = new Label("Enter the weight:");
            lblWeight.setBounds(30, 70, 125, 20);
            txtWeight = new TextField(10);
            txtWeight.setBounds(170, 70, 100, 20);
            add(lblWeight);
            add(txtWeight);
```

```
        lblBreed = new Label("Enter the breed:");
        lblBreed.setBounds(30, 100, 125, 20);
        txtBreed = new TextField(10);
        txtBreed.setBounds(170, 100, 100, 20);
        add(lblBreed);
        add(txtBreed);

        lblColor = new Label("Enter the color:");
        lblColor.setBounds(30, 130, 125, 20);
        txtColor = new TextField(10);
        txtColor.setBounds(170, 130, 100, 20);
        add(lblColor);
        add(txtColor);

        lblSound = new Label("Enter the sound it makes:");
        lblSound.setBounds(30, 160, 125, 20);
        txtSound = new TextField(10);
        txtSound.setBounds(170, 160, 100, 20);
        add(lblSound);
        add(txtSound);
        txtSound.addActionListener(this);
    }

    public void actionPerformed(ActionEvent e)
    {
        w = Integer.parseInt(txtWeight.getText());
        b = txtBreed.getText();
        c = txtColor.getText();
        s = txtSound.getText();
        Pet.setPet(w, b, c, s);
        repaint();
    }

    public void paint (Graphics g)
    {
        g.drawString("The pet's weight is " + Pet.getWeight() + ".", 30,
250);
        g.drawString("The pet's breed is " + Pet.getBreed() + ".", 30,
280);
        g.drawString("The pet's color is " + Pet.getColor() + ".", 30,
310);
        g.drawString("The pet makes this sound: " + Pet.getSound() + ".",
30, 340);
    }

}
```

This applet must be compiled in order to execute.

Step 3: Save Your Program

Once you have finished typing in your code, save it one final time before compiling your program.

Step 4: Compile and Run

Enter the commands necessary to compile and run your program. If errors occur during the compile, check your code, correct any errors, and rerun the program.

Make sure you test your program. This project should execute in a similar manner to Project 8-1. However, you will notice that the code is different. Remember—everyone programs the same solution differently!

Step 5: Review Your Code

Now that your program has run successfully, review your code so that you understand the enhancements used in this project.

The code above is just one example of a pet. Feel free to modify your pet according to your definition of a pet.

1. The constructor from Project 8-2, PetClass.java, is shown below. Explain it in the space following it.

```
public PetClass()
{
        setPet();
}
```

_____

_____

_____

2. When is the constructor performed? Look in the PetTest applet.

_____

_____

_____

3. How does this method of initializing private data members enforce the separation of interface and implementation?

_____

_____

_____

4. Explain the two different setPet methods. How and when are they used?

_____

_____

_____

_____

5. Explain the get methods used in the PetTest paint method. The code is shown below.

```
public void paint (Graphics g)
{
        g.drawString("The pet's weight is " + Pet.getWeight() + ".", 30,
250);
        g.drawString("The pet's breed is " + Pet.getBreed() + ".", 30,
280);
        g.drawString("The pet's color is " + Pet.getColor() + ".", 30,
310);
        g.drawString("The pet makes this sound: " + Pet.getSound() + ".",
30, 340);
}
```

6. When are these get methods called?

7. Explain the difference between the execution of Project 8-1 and Project 8-2.

Your applet probably looks different from Project 8-1. But if it works, it doesn't matter! You now have an idea of the power of constructors and the separation of implementation and interface.

Packaging represents a much easier way to accumulate, or "package," the user-defined classes you create. In the previous project you might have noticed that you could access the PetClass class by simply including it in the same project folder that your main applet "lives" in. However, that is not a very effective way to further separate implementation and interface. In this project, you will see how you can effectively package your classes into a folder that is separate from your applets, yet still access those classes when needed.

You will use the same classes with which you worked in Project 8-2. In this project you will simply package the PetClass class so that it may be used by anyone needing it. You will be presented with two procedures that can be used for packaging your classes; one is Microsoft-specific, the other Sun Java-specific. The compiler that you are using may have its own method. If so, your teacher can introduce you to the method specific to your compiler. If there is any doubt about the method to use, then use the Sun Java command line method, which is the first one you will be shown here.

Step 1: Start Your Compiler

Start your compiler if it is not already running.

Step 2: Open Your Project 8-2 Files

Open your **PetClass.java** and your **PetTest.java** files. Save these two files in a **Proj8_3** project folder. You will also need to modify your PetClass.java file as shown:

```
package com.yourname.lesson8;
```

This line of code should be inserted immediately after your introductory comment lines and before any other lines of code. "Yourname" should be replaced with your last name.

When you run the commands shown in Step 3, then the Java compiler will place the compiled class in this directory path within the "packages" folder. This means that your compiled class will reside at the following location:

```
C:\packages\com\yourname\lesson8
```

The package key word tells the compiler to create all the folders within the packages folder, except for the *packages* folder (that's your responsibility), and to place your compiled class in the last folder, *lesson8*.

In case you're curious, the folder path is usually the reverse of the programmer's company domain name. For example, a class from Microsoft would probably live at the following path:

```
com.ms
```

Step 3: Start a Command Prompt Session

If you are running Windows 9X or NT, click the **Start** button, choose **Programs**, and then click on the **MS-DOS Prompt** or **Command Prompt** options. If you are using another operating system, check with your instructor on how to start a command session.

First, create a folder in the root directory of your C:\ drive called **packages**. If you feel more comfortable doing this through your GUI, then do so.

Second, change your directory to the one in which your PetClass class resides. For example, my PetClass.java file resides in a folder at the following path:

```
C:\My Documents\Java Project Book\Lesson 8\Lesson 8 Projects\Proj8_3
```

Once you are at that directory, type in the following command line, and then press **Enter:**

```
javac -d c:\packages PetClass.java
```

You will know you are successful if you are returned to a command prompt. If you receive an error message stating that the PetClass file could not be read, then you are probably in the wrong directory. Change your prompt to the correct directory and then rerun the above line of code.

If you are using Microsoft J++, simply include your PetClass.java file in your project with the "package" statement, then compile your main applet, PetTest.java. The Microsoft compiler will create the "com" path directly within your project folder instead of in the "packages" folder. The compiler will also compile your PetClass.java file into a "class" file named PetClass.class.

Once it compiles correctly, regardless of the method used, remove the PetClass.java file from your project folder. The PetTest.java file should be the only file left in the project folder.

Step 4: Modify Your PetTest.java File

Now that your PetClass file does not reside in the same directory as your PetTest file, you must modify your PetTest file to import the PetClass.class file. Open your **PetTest.java** file. Modify your code as directed below. Save the applet with the same name, **PetTest.java**, since you have it saved in a separate project file.

```
// Proj8_3

import java.awt.*;
import java.awt.event.*;
import java.applet.Applet;
import com.sestak.lesson8.*;


public class PetTest extends Applet implements ActionListener
{
    private PetClass Pet;

    int w;
    String b, c, s;
    Label lblIntro, lblWeight, lblBreed, lblColor, lblSound;
    TextField txtWeight, txtBreed, txtColor, txtSound;

    public void init()
    {
        Pet = new PetClass();

        setLayout(null);

        lblIntro = new Label("DESCRIBE YOUR PET!");
        lblIntro.setBounds(90, 30, 150, 20);
```

```java
        add(lblIntro);

        lblWeight = new Label("Enter the weight:");
        lblWeight.setBounds(30, 70, 125, 20);
        txtWeight = new TextField(10);
        txtWeight.setBounds(170, 70, 100, 20);
        add(lblWeight);
        add(txtWeight);

        lblBreed = new Label("Enter the breed:");
        lblBreed.setBounds(30, 100, 125, 20);
        txtBreed = new TextField(10);
        txtBreed.setBounds(170, 100, 100, 20);
        add(lblBreed);
        add(txtBreed);

        lblColor = new Label("Enter the color:");
        lblColor.setBounds(30, 130, 125, 20);
        txtColor = new TextField(10);
        txtColor.setBounds(170, 130, 100, 20);
        add(lblColor);
        add(txtColor);

        lblSound = new Label("Enter the sound it makes:");
        lblSound.setBounds(30, 160, 125, 20);
        txtSound = new TextField(10);
        txtSound.setBounds(170, 160, 100, 20);
        add(lblSound);
        add(txtSound);
        txtSound.addActionListener(this);
    }

    public void actionPerformed(ActionEvent e)
    {
        w = Integer.parseInt(txtWeight.getText());
        b = txtBreed.getText();
        c = txtColor.getText();
        s = txtSound.getText();
        Pet.setPet(w, b, c, s);
        repaint();
    }

    public void paint (Graphics g)
    {
        g.drawString("The pet's weight is " + Pet.getWeight() + ".", 30,
250);
        g.drawString("The pet's breed is " + Pet.getBreed() + ".", 30,
280);
        g.drawString("The pet's color is " + Pet.getColor() + ".", 30,
310);
        g.drawString("The pet makes this sound: " + Pet.getSound() + ".",
30, 340);
    }
}
```

Step 5: Save Your Program

When you have completed typing the code, save your program once more before moving on to the next step. You will notice that the fourth import statement is the only change. This should be replaced with the path to where your files are stored, just as this is the path to where mine are stored.

Step 6: Modify Your Autoexec.bat File

With this Sun Java method of packaging your class files, you will need to modify, or add, a *classpath* variable to your autoexec.bat file. Before modifying your autoexec.bat file, ***please*** make sure that you have your teacher's permission! If you are not allowed to make the changes, have your teacher or system administrator make the changes.

The following line of code should be added to the autoexec.bat file:

```
set classpath = c:\packages
```

If this line already exists *without* your new directory, add your new directory to the existing line. The modification would look something like this:

```
set classpath = c:\java\bin;c:\packages
```

If you are using Microsoft J++, you will need to modify the project properties instead of modifying your autoexec.bat file. Click the **Project** option on the menu bar, and then select the **Proj8_3 Properties**. In the dialog box, click the **Classpath** tab. Click the **New** button to the right of the Default path text box. Another dialog box opens, prompting you to enter the default classpath for this project. Once you enter the default path, click **OK**. Then click **OK** again to close the Proj8_3 Properties dialog box.

Step 7: Compile and Run

Enter the commands necessary to compile and run your program. If errors occur during the compile, check your code, correct any errors, and rerun the program.

Remember to save your program any time you make changes!

Your program should *not* visibly work any differently. Any changes made because of the packaging will work behind the scenes. If your program works after you made the changes, the path to your class is correct. If it does not work, the path you entered is incorrect.

Step 8: Explain Your Code

The only difference in this program is the use of packaging. Therefore, let's concentrate on those lines of code.

1. Explain the following line of code:

```
package com.yourname.lesson8;
```

_____

_____

_____

_____

_____

_____

2. Explain the following line of code:

```
javac -d c:\packages PetClass.java
```

_____

_____

_____

_____

_____

3. Explain the following line of code:

```
import com.sestak.lesson8.*;
```

_____

_____

_____

_____

_____

When you're finished, compare your answers with those of your teacher and classmates. Keep working on your ability to analyze Java code. You should now have a pretty good overview of packaging.

PROJECT 8-4: Inheritance—Derived Classes

This project deals with **_inheritance_**. Even though you won't get any money from a rich relative, you will receive access to a rich set of functions that will make your programs dynamic!

In Project 8-1, you created a single, simple class. In this project, you will create a **_superclass_** and then derive a specific class from the base, or superclass. Instead of having a Pet class and then creating an instance of Pet, you will have a Pet class that "spins off" a Dog class, Cat class, and Snake class. You will then instantiate the dog, cat, and snake classes.

A **_superclass_** is usually a generic class from which the **_subclass_** can inherit attributes and methods. You then create instances of the subclass. However, you can still access all the public members in the superclass through its public methods, as well as those of the subclass. The theory is that everything in the superclass is generic. For example, all pets have a name, have a color, have a type (dog, cat, snake, and so on). Then the specific types (dog, cat, snake, and so forth) have additional attributes that only they possess. For example, cats chase mice, dogs eat bones, and so on. The attributes in the subclass become enhanced.

Your superclass will also be defined as an **abstract class**. An abstract class is one from which no objects are instantiated. You can think of these as "blueprints." They form the basis from which subclasses will be derived. The subclasses then are known as **concrete classes** since they will be instantiated.

Finally, you will practice **polymorphism**. Well, actually you will use a method that practices polymorphism. You will define a method in the superclass that will be overwritten in each of the subclasses. The methods have the same signature, but the body of each will differ depending on which type of pet uses the method. Java will "know" which method to perform based on the class using the method. Polymorphism is the same method doing different things depending on the object that calls it—a method of many faces!

You will modify your code from Project 8-2 into classes.

Step 1: Start Your Compiler

Start your compiler if it is not already running.

Step 2: Type in Your Code

You may open previously written Java files and modify them if you desire, or you can type the code that follows from scratch. You will be given the filenames for each. You will also practice the packaging method that you learned in Project 8-3.

The first file you will create is PetClass2.java. This is your abstract superclass for this project. Every other class you create will be derived from this class. Since it is an abstract class, it is not able to be instantiated. Save this file in an additional project folder named **Proj8_4 Classes** with the filename **PetClass2.java**. This is so you do not overwrite the original PetClass.

```java
// Proj8_4 PetClass2
package com.sestak.lesson8;
import java.awt.Graphics;

public abstract class PetClass2
{
    private int weight;
    private String name, breed, color, sound;

    public PetClass2()
    {
        weight = 0;
        name = breed = color = sound = "";
    }

    public PetClass2(int w, String n, String b, String c, String s)
    {
        weight = w;
        name = n;
        breed = b;
        color = c;
```

```java
        sound = s;
    }

    public void setWeight(int w)
    {
        weight = w;
    }

    public void setName(String n)
    {
        name = n;
    }

    public void setBreed(String b)
    {
        breed = b;
    }

    public void setColor(String c)
    {
        color = c;
    }

    public void setSound(String s)
    {
        sound = s;
    }

    public int getWeight()
    {
        return weight;
    }

    public String getName()
    {
        return name;
    }

    public String getBreed()
    {
        return breed;
    }

    public String getColor()
    {
        return color;
    }

    public String getSound()
    {
        return sound;
    }

    public abstract void draw(Graphics g);
}
```

Now, create the DogClass.java file shown below. This is your first concrete subclass for this project. This class will be instantiated. Save this file in your project folder named **Proj8_4 Classes** with the filename **DogClass.java**.

```java
// Proj8_4 DogClass
package com.sestak.lesson8;
import java.awt.Graphics;

public class DogClass extends PetClass2
{
    public DogClass(int w, String n, String b, String c, String s)
    {
        super(w, n, b, c, s);
    }

    public void draw(Graphics g)
    {
        g.drawString("My dog's name is " + getName() + ".", 30, 350);
        g.drawString("My dog is a " + getBreed() + ", " + "and it weighs "
+ getWeight() + " pounds.", 30, 370);
        g.drawString("My dog is " + getColor() + " as if you can't see!",
30, 390);
        g.drawString("My dog sounds like this: " + getSound() + "!", 30,
410);
    }
}
```

This class extends the superclass. It requires its own constructor, while using the constructor of the superclass. Plus it provides its own draw method, overwriting the abstract draw method from the superclass. You will notice that the other subclasses also provide their own draw methods.

Next, create the CatClass.java file, as shown below. This is your second concrete subclass for this project. This class will be instantiated. Save this file in the **Proj8_4 Classes** project folder with the filename **CatClass.java**.

```java
// Proj8_4 CatClass
package com.sestak.lesson8;
import java.awt.Graphics;

public class CatClass extends PetClass2
{
    public CatClass(int w, String n, String b, String c, String s)
    {
        super(w, n, b, c, s);
    }

    public void draw(Graphics g)
    {
        g.drawString("My cat's name is " + getName() + ".", 30, 350);
        g.drawString("My cat is a " + getBreed() + ", " + "and it weighs "
+ getWeight() + " pounds.", 30, 370);
```

```
            g.drawString("My cat is " + getColor() + " as if you can't see!",
30, 390);
            g.drawString("My cat sounds like this: " + getSound() + "!", 30,
410);
    }
}
```

This class is very similar to the `DogClass`, *but* you can add instance variables and methods to this class that will further differentiate it from the `DogClass`.

The next file you create is SnakeClass.java. Okay, if you're not fond of snakes, change it! This is your last concrete subclass for this project. This class will be instantiated. Save this file in the **Proj8_4 Classes** project folder with the filename **SnakeClass.java**.

```
// Proj8_4 SnakeClass
package com.sestak.lesson8;
import java.awt.Graphics;

public class SnakeClass extends PetClass2
{
    public SnakeClass(int w, String n, String b, String c, String s)
    {
        super(w, n, b, c, s);
    }

    public void draw(Graphics g)
    {
        g.drawString("My snake's name is " + getName() + ".", 30, 350);
        g.drawString("My snake is a " + getBreed() + ", " + "and it weighs
" + getWeight() + " pounds.", 30, 370);
        g.drawString("My snake is " + getColor() + " as if you can't
see!", 30, 390);
        g.drawString("My snake sounds like this: " + getSound() + "!", 30,
410);
    }
}
```

Now you have your abstract superclass and your three concrete subclasses. Let's move on to your interface.

Create the PetsTester.java file, as shown below. This is the applet that the users will see as the interface to your classes. Save this file in the **Proj8_4** project folder with the filename **PetsTester.java**.

```
// Proj8_4 PetsTester

import java.awt.*;
import java.awt.event.*;
import java.applet.Applet;
import com.sestak.lesson8.*;


public class PetsTester extends Applet implements ActionListener
{
```

```
Button btnDog, btnCat, btnSnake;
Label lblIntro, lblName, lblWeight, lblBreed, lblColor, lblSound;
TextField txtWeight, txtName, txtBreed, txtColor, txtSound;

int w;
String n, b, c, s;

int petType;

DogClass dog;
CatClass cat;
SnakeClass snake;


public void init()
{
        setLayout(null);

        lblIntro = new Label("SELECT YOUR PET!");
        lblIntro.setBounds(90, 10, 150, 20);
        add(lblIntro);

        btnDog = new Button("Dog");
        btnDog.setBounds(30, 275, 80, 30);
        add(btnDog);
        btnDog.addActionListener(this);

        btnCat = new Button("Cat");
        btnCat.setBounds(120, 275, 80, 30);
        add(btnCat);
        btnCat.addActionListener(this);

        btnSnake = new Button("Snake");
        btnSnake.setBounds(210, 275, 80, 30);
        add(btnSnake);
        btnSnake.addActionListener(this);

        lblWeight = new Label("Enter the weight:");
        lblWeight.setBounds(30, 70, 125, 20);
        txtWeight = new TextField(10);
        txtWeight.setBounds(170, 70, 100, 20);
        add(lblWeight);
        add(txtWeight);

        lblName = new Label("Enter the name:");
        lblName.setBounds(30, 100, 125, 20);
        txtName = new TextField(10);
        txtName.setBounds(170, 100, 100, 20);
        add(lblName);
        add(txtName);

        lblBreed = new Label("Enter the breed:");
        lblBreed.setBounds(30, 130, 125, 20);
        txtBreed = new TextField(10);
```

```
            txtBreed.setBounds(170, 130, 100, 20);
        add(lblBreed);
        add(txtBreed);

        lblColor = new Label("Enter the color:");
        lblColor.setBounds(30, 160, 125, 20);
        txtColor = new TextField(10);
        txtColor.setBounds(170, 160, 100, 20);
        add(lblColor);
        add(txtColor);

        lblSound = new Label("Enter the sound it makes:");
        lblSound.setBounds(30, 190, 125, 20);
        txtSound = new TextField(10);
        txtSound.setBounds(170, 190, 100, 20);
        add(lblSound);
        add(txtSound);
    }

    public void actionPerformed(ActionEvent e)
    {
        if (e.getSource() == btnDog)
        {
            dog = new DogClass(Integer.parseInt(txtWeight.getText()),
txtName.getText(), txtBreed.getText(), txtColor.getText(),
txtSound.getText());
            petType = 0;
        }

        if (e.getSource() == btnCat)
        {
            cat = new CatClass(Integer.parseInt(txtWeight.getText()),
txtName.getText(), txtBreed.getText(), txtColor.getText(),
txtSound.getText());
            petType = 1;
        }

        if (e.getSource() == btnSnake)
        {
            snake = new
SnakeClass(Integer.parseInt(txtWeight.getText()), txtName.getText(),
txtBreed.getText(), txtColor.getText(), txtSound.getText());
            petType = 2;
        }

        repaint();
    }

    public void paint (Graphics g)
    {
        switch (petType)
        {
        case 0:
            dog.draw(g);
            break;
```

```
        case 1:
                cat.draw(g);
                break;

        case 2:
                snake.draw(g);
                break;
        }
    }
}
```

Once you get this typed in and saved, you will need to package your other classes.

Step 3: Package Your Classes

Using the method described in Project 8-3, package each of the classes saved in your **Proj8_4 Classes** folder. You will package these classes to the *same* **packages** folder used in Project 8-3.

Step 4: Compile and Run

Enter the commands necessary to compile your program. If errors occur during the compile, check your code, correct any errors, and rerun the program.

Your new program should be similar to the earlier projects in this lesson. However, you now have three command buttons to use to instantiate the "proper" pet type based on the information you have entered.

Step 5: Review Your Code

Now that your program has run successfully, review your code with your classmates and teacher.

1. In the space below, explain the following block of code:

```
// Proj8_4 PetClass2
package com.sestak.lesson8;
import java.awt.Graphics;
```

_____

_____

_____

_____

_____

_____

2. What is the purpose of the following block of code?

```
public abstract class PetClass2
{
    private int weight;
    private String name, breed, color, sound;
```

_____

_____

_____

_____

_____

_____

3. Explain the following blocks of code. Compare their purposes.

```java
public PetClass2()
{
    weight = 0;
    name = breed = color = sound = "";
}

public PetClass2(int w, String n, String b, String c, String s)
{
    weight = w;
    name = n;
    breed = b;
    color = c;
    sound = s;
}
```

_____

_____

_____

_____

_____

4. Summarize the purpose of the set and get methods from PetClass2.java.

_____

_____

_____

_____

_____

5. Explain the following abstract method:

```java
public abstract void draw(Graphics g);
```

_____

_____

_____

_____

6. Explain the following block of code:

```
// Proj8_4 DogClass
package com.sestak.lesson8;
import java.awt.Graphics;
```

7. Explain the following subclass constructor:

```
public class DogClass extends PetClass2
{
    public DogClass(int w, String n, String b, String c, String s)
    {
        super(w, n, b, c, s);
    }
```

8. Explain the following overwritten method:

```
public void draw(Graphics g
    {
        g.drawString("My dog's name is " + getName() + ".", 30, 350);
        g.drawString("My dog is a " + getBreed() + ", " + "and it weighs "
+ getWeight() + " pounds.", 30, 370);
        g.drawString("My dog is " + getColor() + " as if you can't see!",
30, 390);
        g.drawString("My dog sounds like this: " + getSound() + "!", 30,
410);
    }
```

_____

_____

_____

_____

9. Explain the following declarations from the PetsTester class:

```
int w;
String n, b, c, s;

int petType;

DogClass dog;
CatClass cat;
SnakeClass snake;
```

_____

_____

_____

_____

_____

10. Explain the following block of code from the PetsTester class:

```
public void actionPerformed(ActionEvent e)
{
        if (e.getSource() == btnDog)
        {
                dog = new DogClass(Integer.parseInt(txtWeight.getText()),
txtName.getText(), txtBreed.getText(), txtColor.getText(),
txtSound.getText()));
                petType = 0;
        }
```

_____

_____

_____

_____

_____

11. Explain the paint method from the PetsTester class:

```
public void paint (Graphics g)
{
        switch (petType)
        {
```

```
case 0:
        dog.draw(g);
        break;

case 1:
        cat.draw(g);
        break;

case 2:
        snake.draw(g);
        break;
    }
}
```

_____

_____

_____

_____

_____

12. Explain the polymorphic behavior of the draw method from the block of code above.

_____

_____

_____

_____

_____

_____

The benefit of using superclasses and subclasses will become more apparent as you derive more and more classes off of the superclass.

Summary

Classes are powerful objects. You can now define objects that you need for your programs. You are no longer limited to using what is provided to you.

In this lesson, you created a single, simple class. From that single class, you learned how to utilize constructors. You explored the concept of inheritance. By creating a superclass and then deriving a class from the superclass, you can create a multitude of objects that can reuse various attributes and methods of classes above it. Classes, as you've probably realized, are an integral part of Java.

You also learned how to package the classes you create and how to import them into other applets. This allows you to further separate interface and implementation of your code.

Finally, you learned how to create multiple subclasses. By incorporating abstract functions into your superclass and overwriting the abstract functions in your subclasses, you can leave it up to the program to find the proper function to use. This is the nature of polymorphism. Now you can create objects that perform as you need them to!

SHORT ANSWER

Define the following in the space provided.

1. Classes

   _____

   _____

   _____

2. Objects

   _____

   _____

   _____

3. Data types

   _____

   _____

   _____

4. Methods

   _____

   _____

   _____

5. Constructor

   _____

   _____

   _____

6. User-defined data type

   _____

   _____

   _____

7. Inheritance

   _____

   _____

   _____

8. Superclass

_____

_____

_____

9. Subclass

_____

_____

_____

10. Aggregate data type

_____

_____

_____

11. Abstract function

_____

_____

_____

12. Encapsulation

_____

_____

_____

13. Object-oriented programming

_____

_____

_____

14. Instance variables

_____

_____

_____

15. Interface

_____

_____

_____

16. Implementation

_____

_____

_____

17. Derive

_____

_____

_____

18. Import

_____

_____

_____

19. Package

_____

_____

_____

20. Classpath

_____

_____

_____

21. Abstract class

_____

_____

_____

22. Concrete class

_____

_____

_____

23. Polymorphism

_____

_____

_____

24. Overwriting

_____

_____

_____

WRITTEN QUESTIONS

Write your answers to the following questions in the space provided.

1. Define _class._

_____

_____

_____

2. Why should instance variables be defined as private?

_____

_____

_____

3. Why should methods be public?

_____

_____

_____

4. Explain what is meant by separating interface and implementation.

_____

_____

_____

5. Explain the differences between a superclass and a subclass.

_____

_____

_____

_____

_____

6. Explain abstract functions.

_____

_____

_____

7. Explain the difference between an abstract class and a concrete class.

_____

_____

_____

_____

_____

8. Explain the benefits of using classes.

_____

_____

_____

_____

_____

9. Explain the overwriting of methods.

_____

_____

_____

_____

_____

10. Explain the process of packaging classes.

_____

_____

_____

_____

_____

_____

_____

_____

11. Explain when and when not to use the import statement, as it relates to the use of other classes.

_____

_____

_____

_____

TESTING YOUR SKILLS

⏱ Estimated Time:

Application 8-1 3 hours
Application 8-2 1 ¹/₂ hours

APPLICATION 8-1

In Project 8-2, you coded PetClass and a PetTester interface. In this application, you're going to add the ability to that class and interface for your Pet to ask for food.

The applet should work like this: When you are creating your Pet, in this case a dog, you will add the ability to give your pet some bones. Based on the number of bones you enter, your dog will tell you whether or not it is hungry! Obviously, if your dog has no bones, it will be hungry. Otherwise, it will not be hungry.

Open the **PetClass.java** file and the **PetTest.java** file. Save them both in an **App8_1 folder**. You can save them with their original names since they will be in a different folder. Add the necessary instance variables and methods to your class. Add the needed interface objects to your PetTest code.

APPLICATION 8-2

This application will expand on Project 8-4. You will add another subclass to Project 8-4. Open your existing Project 8-4 files and save them in an **App8_2 folder** so that you do not overwrite the originals.

Make this new subclass a bird subclass. Package the subclass in the **packages** folder on your hard drive.

CRITICAL THINKING

⏱ Estimated Time: 8–10 hours

Using the techniques covered in this lesson, create a virtual zoo. The zoo will be built out of an animal superclass (all animals have similar basic traits). Then each animal housed in the zoo will become a subclass. If you have more than one type of animal, you will have multiple instances. Each specific type of animal will possess traits specific to it and will do things (methods) specific to its type.

You can make this as easy or as complex as you wish. On the easy end, you can simply create multiple pet-style subclasses. On the complex end, you can have the animals interact with each other. For example, the lion would probably eat the deer!

GRAPHICAL USER INTERFACES

On completion of this lesson, you should be able to:

- Use the various layout managers.

- Add GUI components to layouts.

- Use GUI components.

- Handle mouse events.

- Handle keyboard events.

 Estimated Time: 12 hours

Introduction

In this lesson, you will learn more about *layout managers* and *GUI components*. You will begin with the default layout manager, *FlowLayout*, and the use of the more common GUI components—*buttons* and *labels*. You can think of this as a review and reinforcement. From there you will remove the layout manager so that you, the programmer, can take control.

You will also revisit the *GridLayout* layout manager. You will recall that the GridLayout aligns your components in rows and columns. You will also be introduced to the *Checkbox* class, which will be used to create *check boxes* and *radio buttons*.

The third layout manager that you will use is the *BorderLayout*. The BorderLayout arranges components into five regions: *NORTH*, *SOUTH*, *EAST*, *WEST*, and *CENTER*. The various layout managers will provide you with a great deal of control over the layout of your applet. The various components give you a variety of tools from which to choose.

You will also experiment with *mouse events* and *keyboard events*. Mouse events consist of *pressing*, *clicking*, *releasing*, *entering*, *exiting*, *dragging*, and *moving*. When you perform these common mouse actions, you can program your applet to respond to those actions. The keyboard events respond to keys being pressed and released on the keyboard. You will write code that will respond to *pressing*, *typing*, or *releasing* a key on the keyboard.

This lesson will focus on the following:

- **Using the various layout managers.** This will be a review of the layout managers used in earlier projects, as well as an introduction to the other layout managers. You will work with the FlowLayout, GridLayout, and BorderLayout, and you will remove the default layout manager so that you can control component placement yourself.

- **Adding and using various GUI components.** You will be using the Label, Button, and TextField controls from earlier lessons. And you will be adding the Checkbox, TextArea, and List components to your repertoire.

- **Handling mouse events.** You will be coding applets that respond to your mouse activities. When you perform these events your applet will perform in response.

- **Handling keyboard events.** In addition to mouse events, you will code your applet to respond to different keys being pressed, typed, or released. It's important to know how to respond to both types of events in case a user loses mouse control or is not able to use a mouse.

PROJECT 9-1:
FlowLayout, Buttons, and Labels   Ⓑ

You will begin this lesson with a simple applet that reinforces the components used in previous lessons. The FlowLayout layout manager, which is the default layout manager, will provide the layout rules for your applet. FlowLayout causes the GUI components to be placed onto your **container** from left to right in the order in which they are added. When they reach the edge of the applet they continue on the next line.

In this project, you will be creating a simple applet that uses buttons to change the text of a corresponding label. The main focus of this project is to understand how the FlowLayout layout manager works.

Step 1: Start Your Compiler

Start your compiler if it is not already running.

Step 2: Type in Your Code

Type in your code as follows. Save the file as **Proj9_1.java**.

```
// Proj9_1 FlowLayout, buttons, labels

import java.awt.*;
import java.awt.event.*;
import java.applet.Applet;


public class Proj9_1 extends Applet implements ActionListener
{
    Button button1, button2;
    Label label1, label2;

    public void init()
    {
        button1 = new Button("Display Label 1");
        add(button1);
        button1.addActionListener(this);
```

```
        label1 = new Label("");
        add(label1);

        button2 = new Button("Display Label 2");
        add(button2);
        button2.addActionListener(this);

        label2 = new Label("");
        add(label2);
    }

    public void actionPerformed(ActionEvent e)
    {
        if (e.getSource() == button1)
        {
            label1.setText("You clicked button 1!");
            label1.show();
            showStatus(label1.getText());
            label2.hide();
        }

        if (e.getSource() == button2)
        {
            label2.setText("You clicked button 2!");
            label2.show();
            showStatus(label2.getText());
            label1.hide();
        }
    }
}
```

Step 3: Save Your Program

Once you have finished typing in your code, save it one final time before compiling your program.

Step 4: Compile and Run

Enter the commands necessary to compile and run your program. If errors occur during the compile, check your code, correct any errors, and rerun the program.

Execute this applet at various sizes to see what problems you encounter with the placement of the components. Then, execute this applet maximized. Make sure you understand the execution of the FlowLayout layout manager.

Your applet should look similar to Figure 9-1.

FIGURE 9-1
Project 9-1 applet

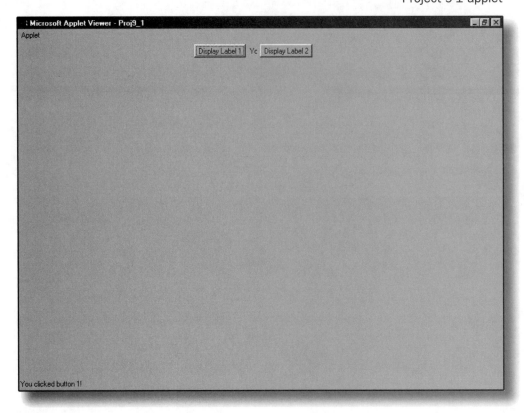

Step 5: Review Your Code

Now that your program has run successfully, experiment with it so you gain an understanding of how it executes. Once you feel comfortable with the execution, answer the questions below.

1. Explain what happens when either of the buttons is clicked.

_____

_____

_____

_____

_____

_____

2. Explain why neither of the labels is fully displayed.

_____

_____

_____

3. Write the text that should be displayed in each label.

_____

_____

_____

4. Explain why the buttons are so close to each other and why they do not provide enough space for the labels.

_____

_____

_____

_____

_____

_____

_____

5. Explain what happens when the applet is executed at various sizes.

_____

_____

_____

_____

_____

_____

_____

6. Describe two methods for correcting this situation, other than displaying the label text in the status window.

_____

_____

_____

_____

_____

_____

_____

7. Explain the execution of the FlowLayout layout manager.

_____

_____

_____

8. The hide and show methods have been deprecated. Explain what that means.

_____

_____

_____

_____

_____

_____

9. The setVisible(boolean) method has replaced the hide and show methods. Explain the execution of this method.

_____

_____

_____

_____

_____

You have reviewed the use of the default layout manager and the button and label GUI components. You will correct the execution of this applet in the end-of-lesson applications.

P R O J E C T   9 - 2 : Removing the Layout Manager Ⓑ

As you discovered in the previous project, the FlowLayout layout manager may cause problems with your layout. The reason is that the GUI components are added left to right until the edge of the container is reached, and then the components move down to the beginning of the next line. Using the default layout manager is not going to provide you with a great deal of control.

In this project, you will remove the layout manager from governing the layout of your applet. You will set the layout manager to *null* and then set the placement of each of your components. You will use the *setBounds* method, as you have in previous projects, to place your components in specific locations.

Instead of working with buttons and labels in this project, you will be working with TextField controls and will be introduced to the Checkbox class. You will be using the *Checkbox* component to add *"normal" check boxes* to your applet. The "normal" check boxes allow multiple selections. You will use Checkbox to create *radio button* check boxes in the next project.

You will also be introduced to another type of *interface* in this project—the *ItemListener*. The ItemListener interface handles item events generated by a Checkbox control. When a check box is checked, the *itemStateChanged* method is called. The code within this method is then executed based upon which item was selected.

You will use the various components in this project to create an applet similar to, but better organized than, the one in Project 9-1.

Step 1: Start Your Compiler

Start your compiler if it is not already running.

Step 2: Type in Your Code

Type in the code as follows. Save the file as **Proj9_2.java**.

```java
// Proj9_2 Null layout manager, checkboxes, textfields

import java.awt.*;
import java.awt.event.*;
import java.applet.Applet;


public class Proj9_2 extends Applet implements ItemListener
{
    Checkbox cb1, cb2;
    TextField tf1, tf2;

    public void init()
    {
        setLayout(null);

        cb1 = new Checkbox("Display TextField 1");
        cb1.setBounds(30, 30, 150, 20);
        add(cb1);
        cb1.addItemListener(this);

        tf1 = new TextField();
        tf1.setBounds(220, 30, 200, 20);
        add(tf1);

        cb2 = new Checkbox("Display TextField 2");
        cb2.setBounds(30, 60, 150, 20);
        add(cb2);
        cb2.addItemListener(this);

        tf2 = new TextField();
        tf2.setBounds(220, 60, 200, 20);
        add(tf2);
    }

    public void itemStateChanged(ItemEvent e)
    {
        if (cb1.getState() == true)
        {
            tf1.setVisible(true);
            tf1.setText("You checked checkbox 1!");
        }

        if (cb1.getState() == false)
        {
            tf1.setVisible(false);
            tf1.setText("");
        }

        if (cb2.getState() == true)
        {
```

```
                tf2.setVisible(true);
                tf2.setText("You checked checkbox 2!");
        }

        if (cb2.getState() == false)
        {
                tf2.setVisible(false);
                tf2.setText("");
        }

    }
}
```

Step 3: Save Your Program

Once you have finished typing in your code, save it one final time before compiling your program.

Step 4: Compile and Run

Enter the commands necessary to compile and run your program. If errors occur during the compile, check your code, correct any errors, and rerun the program.

Make sure you test your program. Run this applet maximized. You will see two check boxes (the normal ones that allow multiple selections). When a check box is selected, the corresponding text field will appear. When the check box is unselected, the corresponding text field disappears.

Your applet should look similar to Figure 9-2.

FIGURE 9-2
Project 9-2 applet

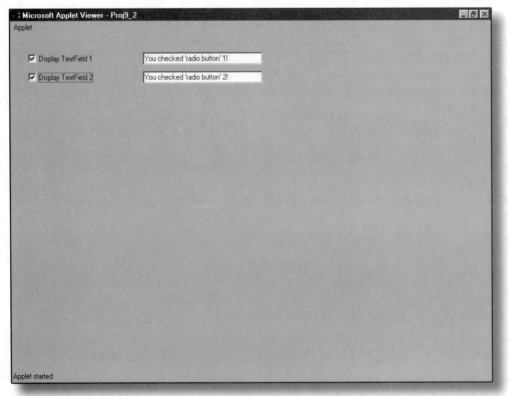

Step 5: Review Your Code

Now that your program has run successfully, review your code so that you understand the enhancements used in this project.

This applet is similar to the applet you created in Project 9-1. However, you used different components with no layout manager.

1. Explain what happens when either of the check boxes is selected.

_____

_____

_____

2. Explain what happens when both check boxes are selected. Explain why this is possible.

_____

_____

_____

_____

_____

_____

3. Write the text that should be displayed in each text field.

_____

_____

_____

4. Explain why the components are aligned neatly in this applet.

_____

_____

_____

5. Explain what happens when the applet is executed at various sizes.

_____

_____

_____

6. Explain the ItemListener interface.

_____

_____

_____

_____

_____

7. Explain the execution of the itemStateChanged method.

_____

_____

_____

_____

8. Explain the execution of the setVisible(boolean) method.

_____

_____

_____

_____

9. Explain the execution of the getState() method.

_____

_____

_____

_____

_____

10. Explain why the following sequence of code is necessary:

```
if (cb1.getState() == true)
{
    tf1.setVisible(true);
    tf1.setText("You checked checkbox 1!");
}

if (cb1.getState() == false)
{
    tf1.setVisible(false);
    tf1.setText("");
}
```

_____

_____

_____

_____

_____

_____

Your applet probably looks different from the one you created in Project 9-1, but it should execute in a similar manner. The major differences between the two are that this project used different components and allowed you to control the layout.

P R O J E C T   9 - 3 :
GridLayout, Radio Buttons, and Labels

Ⓑ

You used the *GridLayout manager* in an earlier lesson. We will revisit the GridLayout here as another method with which to control the layout of the components on your applet. You will align your components in rows and columns.

You will also use the check boxes as *radio buttons* (single-selection check boxes). Instead of being able to make multiple selections, you will now only be able to make one choice from those offered. You will use the radio buttons to change the font properties of labels.

Step 1: Start Your Compiler

Start your compiler if it is not already running.

Step 2: Type in Your Code

Type in your code as follows. Save the file as **Proj9_3.java**.

```java
// Proj9_3 GridLayout manager, radio buttons, labels

import java.awt.*;
import java.awt.event.*;
import java.applet.Applet;


public class Proj9_3 extends Applet implements ItemListener
{
    Font fBold, fItal;
    CheckboxGroup fontStyle;
    Checkbox cb1, cb2;
    Label label1, label2;

    public void init()
    {
        setLayout(new GridLayout(2, 2, 5, 5));

        fontStyle = new CheckboxGroup();

        cb1 = new Checkbox("Bold", fontStyle, false);
```

```
            add(cb1);
            cb1.addItemListener(this);

            cb2 = new Checkbox("Italics", fontStyle, false);
            add(cb2);
            cb2.addItemListener(this);

            label1 = new Label("Watch me change!");
            add(label1);

            label2 = new Label("No! Watch me change!");
            add(label2);

            fBold = new Font("Serif", Font.BOLD, 12);
            fItal = new Font("Serif", Font.ITALIC, 12);
    }

    public void itemStateChanged(ItemEvent e)
    {
            if (e.getSource() == cb1)
            {
                    label1.setFont(fBold);
                    label2.setFont(fBold);
                    showStatus("You checked 'radio button' 1!");
            }

            if (e.getSource() == cb2)
            {
                    label1.setFont(fItal);
                    label2.setFont(fItal);
                    showStatus("You checked 'radio button' 2!");
            }
    }
}
```

Step 3: Save Your Program

Once you have finished typing in your code, save it one final time before compiling your program.

Step 4: Compile and Run

Enter the commands necessary to compile and run your program. If errors occur during the compile, check your code, correct any errors, and rerun the program.

Make sure you test your program. Run this applet maximized. You will see two radio buttons (notice that they are round). When a radio button is selected, the corresponding label will have its text modified. You will also notice that the radio button selection causes the status window to notify you which button was selected. In this applet you cannot select more than one button.

Your applet should look similar to Figure 9-3.

FIGURE 9-3
Project 9-3 applet

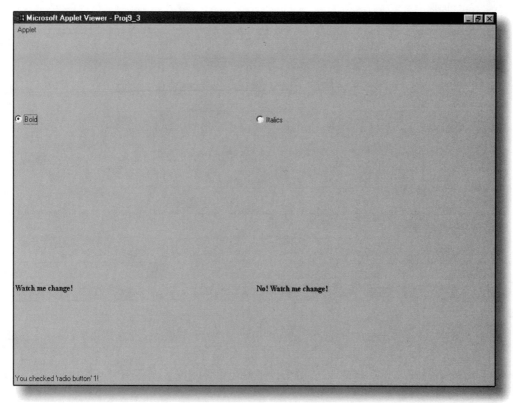

Step 5: Review Your Code

Now that your program has run successfully, review your code so that you understand the enhancements used in this project.

1. Explain what happens when either of the radio buttons is selected.

_____

_____

_____

2. Explain what happens when you attempt to click both radio buttons.

_____

_____

_____

3. Explain why the normal check box is square and the radio button is round.

_____

_____

_____

217

4. Explain how this falls under the concept of user-friendly.

_____

_____

_____

5. Explain why the components are aligned neatly in this applet.

_____

_____

_____

6. Explain what happens when the applet is executed at various sizes.

_____

_____

_____

7. Explain why the getSource method works in this applet.

_____

_____

_____

8. Explain the CheckboxGroup object.

_____

_____

_____

9. Explain the following line of code:

```
setLayout(new GridLayout(2, 2, 5, 5));
```

_____

_____

_____

_____

_____

_____

10. Explain the following line of code:

```
cb2 = new Checkbox("Italics", fontStyle, false);
```

_____

_____

_____

_____

_____

_____

_____

11. Explain the following lines of code:

```
fBold = new Font("Serif", Font.BOLD, 12);
fItal = new Font("Serif", Font.ITALIC, 12);
```

_____

_____

_____

_____

_____

_____

_____

12. Explain the following lines of code and how they relate to the lines of code in Question 11:

```
label1.setFont(fBold);
label1.setFont(fItal);
```

_____

_____

_____

_____

_____

_____

_____

You have now used multiple layout managers and multiple components in your applets.

This project introduces the **BorderLayout** layout manager. The BorderLayout layout manager arranges components into five regions: **North**, **South**, **East, West,** and **Center**. One component is added to each of the regions.

The North and South regions will expand from one side of the applet to the other side. The East and West regions will expand vertically between the North and South regions, if they are present. If not, they will expand from the top to the bottom of the applet. The East and West regions are as wide as the component placed in those regions. However, they will not become any wider, even if the Center region is missing. The Center region expands to take all remaining space.

In this project you will use the BorderLayout manager to organize your components. You will add **TextArea** controls to four of the regions and then use a button to copy text between areas. A text area is similar to a **text field** since they both inherit from **TextComponent**. However, remember that subclasses do not contain all the same methods or properties even if they do inherit from the same superclass. Text areas can be much larger than text fields, can have scrollbars, and can be set to automatically **word wrap**. You will use text areas to input and copy text.

HOT TIP

The names of the regions *must* be typed in all CAPS.

Step 1: Start Your Compiler

Start your compiler if it is not already running.

Step 2: Type in Your Code

Type in your code as follows. Save the file as **Proj9_4.java**.

```
// Proj9_4 BorderLayout manager, text areas

import java.awt.*;
import java.awt.event.*;
import java.applet.Applet;


public class Proj9_4 extends Applet implements ActionListener
{
    TextArea ta1, ta2, ta3, ta4;
    Button btnCopy;

    public void init()
    {
        setLayout(new BorderLayout(5, 5));

        ta1 = new TextArea(5, 20);
        add(ta1, BorderLayout.NORTH);

        ta2 = new TextArea(5, 20);
```

```
        add(ta2, BorderLayout.SOUTH);

        ta3 = new TextArea(5, 20);
        add(ta3, BorderLayout.WEST);

        ta4 = new TextArea(5, 20);
        add(ta4, BorderLayout.EAST);

        btnCopy = new Button("Copy Selected Text From North To West, From
South To East");
        add(btnCopy, BorderLayout.CENTER);
        btnCopy.addActionListener(this);
    }

    public void actionPerformed(ActionEvent e)
    {
        ta3.setText(ta1.getSelectedText());
        ta4.setText(ta2.getSelectedText());
    }
}
```

Step 3: Save Your Program

Once you have finished typing in your code, save it one final time before compiling your program.

Step 4: Compile and Run

Enter the commands necessary to compile and run your program. If errors occur during the compile, check your code, correct any errors, and rerun the program.

Make sure you test your program. Run this applet maximized. You will see the five components and the border regions that they occupy. When text is typed into the North text area and then highlighted, clicking the button will cause it to be copied into the West text area. The same is true of text typed into the South text area, except that it will be copied into the East text area. Highlighting text in both the North and South text areas will cause both sections of highlighted text to be copied at the same time. You will also notice that the button, which occupies the Center region, is very large since it expands to fill the rest of the available space.

One last thing to notice: If the text that you copy from the North or South regions is too long for the East or West text areas, scrollbars will automatically appear on that text area so that you may view the entire text. This is a significant difference between a text area and a text field.

Your applet should look similar to Figure 9-4.

FIGURE 9-4
Project 9-4 applet

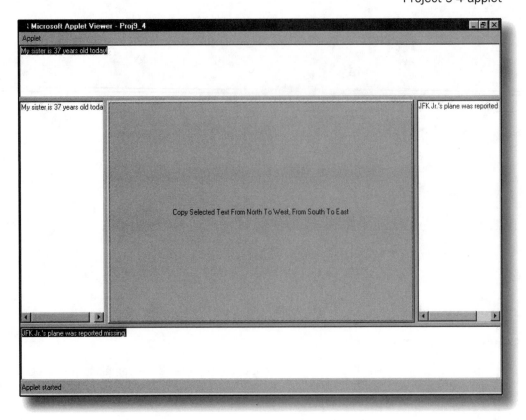

Step 5: Review Your Code

Now that your program has run successfully, review your code so that you understand the enhancements used in this project.

1. Explain what happens when the button is clicked and no text in the North or South text areas is highlighted versus text being highlighted.

_____

_____

_____

2. Explain the BorderLayout layout manager.

_____

_____

3. Explain why the text areas in the North and South regions expand horizontally and the East and West text areas do not when they are all instantiated with the same attributes.

_____

_____

_____

_____

_____

_____

4. How many components can be added to each region? Explain why.

_____

_____

_____

5. Explain the following line of code:

```
setLayout(new BorderLayout(5, 5));
```

_____

_____

_____

6. Explain the following line of code:

```
ta1 = new TextArea(5, 20);
```

_____

_____

_____

7. Explain the following line of code.

```
add(ta1, BorderLayout.NORTH);
```

_____

_____

_____

8. Explain what will happen if the names of the regions are not typed in all caps.

_____

_____

_____

9. Explain the following line of code.

```
ta3.setText(ta1.getSelectedText());
```

_____

_____

_____

10. Explain the difference between a text field and a text area.

_____

_____

_____

_____

_____

_____

You have now learned how to use a brand-new layout manager and another useful component that can be utilized in other applets.

PROJECT 9-5 : Mouse Events (B)

This project deals with simple **mouse events**. Mouse events occur when the mouse is used. Mouse events can be used for any component that derives from **Component**. Each mouse event method takes a **MouseEvent** object as its argument. A MouseEvent object contains information about the type of event that occurred and the **x** and **y coordinates** at which it happened.

You will use the following methods in regard to mouse events:

- **mousePressed**—called when the mouse is pressed with the pointer over a component.

- **mouseClicked**—called when a mouse button is released without moving the mouse after a mousePressed event.

- **mouseReleased**—called when the mouse is released after a dragging event.

- **mouseEntered**—called when the mouse enters the boundaries of a component.

- **mouseExited**—called when the mouse leaves the boundaries of a component.

- **mouseDragged**—called when the mouse button is pressed and held and the mouse is moved (dragged). The mouseDragged method is "sandwiched" between the mousePressed and mouseReleased methods.

- **mouseMoved**—called when the mouse is moved with the mouse cursor over a component.

You will use each of these methods in this project. By using and comparing these methods within the same applet, you will be able to better understand how they execute and how they relate to one another.

Because you are using all these methods, you will need to implement both the **MouseListener** and **MouseMotionListener** interfaces. When a class implements both interfaces, the programmer must define all seven methods.

Step 1: Start Your Compiler

Start your compiler if it is not already running.

Step 2: Type in Your Code

Type in your code as follows. Save the file as **Proj9_5.java**.

```java
// Proj9_5 Mouse events

import java.awt.*;
import java.awt.event.*;
import java.applet.Applet;


public class Proj9_5 extends Applet implements MouseListener,
MouseMotionListener
{
    private int xpos, ypos = -5;
    private String action = "";

    public void init()
    {
        addMouseListener(this);
        addMouseMotionListener(this);
    }

    public void paint(Graphics g)
    {
        g.drawString(action + " @ (" + xpos + ", " + ypos +")", xpos,
ypos);
    }

    public void setDrawString(String a, int x, int y)
    {
        action = a;
        xpos = x;
        ypos = y;
        repaint();
    }

    public void mouseClicked(MouseEvent e)
    {
        setDrawString("Clicked", e.getX(), e.getY());
    }

    public void mousePressed(MouseEvent e)
    {
        setDrawString("Pressed", e.getX(), e.getY());
    }

    public void mouseReleased(MouseEvent e)
    {
        setDrawString("Released", e.getX(), e.getY());
    }

    public void mouseEntered(MouseEvent e)
    {
```

```
        setDrawString("Entered", e.getX(), e.getY());
}

public void mouseExited(MouseEvent e)
{
        setDrawString("Exited", e.getX(), e.getY());
}

public void mouseDragged(MouseEvent e)
{
        setDrawString("Dragged", e.getX(), e.getY());
}

public void mouseMoved(MouseEvent e)
{
        setDrawString("Moving", e.getX(), e.getY());
}
}
```

Step 3: Save Your Program

Once you have finished typing in your code, save it one final time before compiling your program.

Step 4: Compile and Run

Enter the commands necessary to compile and run your program. If errors occur during the compile, check your code, correct any errors, and rerun the program.

Make sure you test your program. Run this applet at various sizes. You will see the mouse events and the coordinates at which the events occur displayed on the face of your applet. Experiment with the events. Review the introduction to this project on how the various events execute. This way you will be able to make sure that you are causing the mouse to perform the events that will trigger the applet display.

Run your applet at a size similar to Figure 9-5. The various events will display on the face of your applet.

FIGURE 9-5
Project 9-5 applet

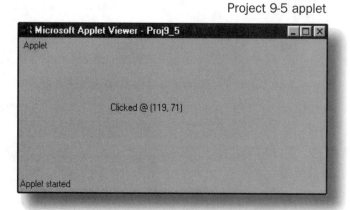

Step 5: Review Your Code

Now that your program has run successfully, review your code so that you understand the enhancements used in this project.

1. Explain why the applet face is initially blank.

_____

_____

_____

2. Explain which event is hard to see.

_____

_____

3. Explain the difference between MouseListener and MouseMotionListener interfaces.

_____

_____

4. Explain why each of the methods must be defined when implementing both of the above interfaces.

_____

_____

5. Explain the purpose of setting the initial *x* and *y* coordinates at negative positions.

_____

_____

6. Identify which component the mouse listeners have been added to.

_____

_____

7. Explain the purpose of the setDrawString method.

_____

_____

_____

_____

8. Explain how the setDrawString method interfaces with the mouse events.

_____

_____

_____

_____

_____

9. Explain the following line of code:

```
        g.drawString(action + " @ (" + xpos + ", " + ypos +")", xpos,
ypos);
```

_____

_____

_____

_____

10. Explain the following line of code:

```
setDrawString("Clicked", e.getX(), e.getY());
```

_____

_____

_____

_____

Mouse events will prove to be very useful in your programming career. You now have a basic understanding of how they execute.

P R O J E C T 9 - 6 : Keyboard Events Ⓑ

The last topic you will be introduced to in this lesson is **keyboard events**. You might be thinking of what use keyboard events are when most people use a mouse. Keep in mind that not everyone is physically capable of using a mouse; some people are actually forced into relying on the keyboard. With this in mind you should write all of your programs so that they are accessible by both mouse interface _and_ keyboard interface. Providing access by both mouse and keyboard is a major component of user-friendliness.

Key events are generated when the user presses keys on the keyboard. The following methods are executed in response to key events:

- **keyPressed**—called in response to pressing an **action key**. Action keys are the arrow keys, function keys, and the Home, End, Page Up, Page Down, Num Lock, Print Screen, Scroll Lock, Caps Lock, and Pause keys.

- **keyTyped**—called in response to any other key being pressed.

- **keyReleased**—called in response to any key being released after a keyPressed or keyTyped event.

- The **KeyListener interface** handles key events. Any class that implements this interface must provide definitions for the three methods described above.

Step 1: Start Your Compiler

Start your compiler if it is not already running.

Step 2: Type in Your Code

Type in your code as follows. Save the file as **Proj9_6.java**.

```java
// Proj9_6 Keyboard events

import java.awt.*;
import java.awt.event.*;
import java.applet.Applet;


public class Proj9_6 extends Applet implements KeyListener
{
    Label label1, label2, label3;

    public void init()
    {
        setLayout(null);

        label1 = new Label();
        label1.setBounds(30, 30, 200, 20);
        add(label1);

        label2 = new Label();
        label2.setBounds(30, 60, 200, 20);
        add(label2);

        label3 = new Label();
        label3.setBounds(30, 90, 200, 20);
        add(label3);

        addKeyListener(this);
        requestFocus();
    }

    public void keyPressed(KeyEvent e)
    {
        label1.setText("Key Pressed: " + e.getKeyText(e.getKeyCode()));
        label2.setText("This key " + (e.isActionKey() ? " is " : " is not
") + "an action key.");
        label3.setText("Try another key!!");
        repaint();
    }

    public void keyTyped(KeyEvent e)
    {
        label1.setText("Key Typed: " + e.getKeyChar());
        label2.setText("This key " + (e.isActionKey() ? " is " : " is not
") + "an action key.");
        label3.setText("Try another key!!");
        repaint();
    }

    public void keyReleased(KeyEvent e)
    {
        label1.setText("Key Released: " + e.getKeyText(e.getKeyCode()));
```

229

```
            label2.setText("This key " + (e.isActionKey() ? " is " : " is not
") + "an action key.");
            label3.setText("Try another key!!");
            repaint();
    }
}
```

Step 3: Save Your Program

Once you have finished typing in your code, save it one final time before compiling your program.

Step 4: Compile and Run

Enter the commands necessary to compile and run your program. If errors occur during the compile, check your code, correct any errors, and rerun the program.

Make sure you test your program. Run this applet maximized. You will see a blank applet when it first begins. The reason is that your labels have no text assigned to them. Once you begin pressing/typing keys the label text will be displayed. One of the first things you will notice is that when you press/type the key, the applet will display the "Released" message. That is because every time you press/type a key you normally release it. In order to see which method is being called you need to hold the key down to see the specific message.

The next thing you will notice is that the second label displays the type of key that you pressed/typed. If you "pressed" a key, which means it is an action key, you will be told that it is an action key. If you "typed" a normal key, the message will tell you that it is not an action key.

Your applet should look similar to Figure 9-6.

FIGURE 9-6
Project 9-6 applet

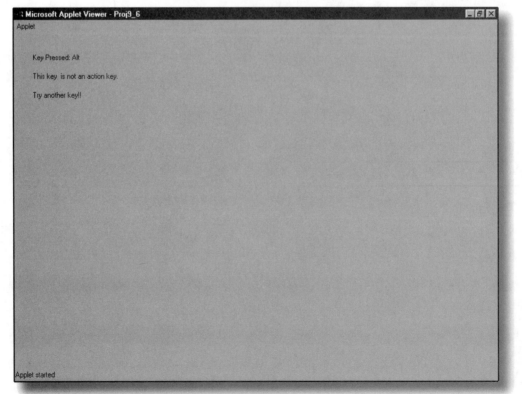

Step 5: Review Your Code

Now that your program has run successfully, review your code so that you understand the enhancements used in this project.

1. Explain what happens when a letter key is pressed.

_____

_____

_____

2. Explain what happens when an action key is pressed.

_____

_____

_____

3. Explain which method is performed with each type of key.

_____

_____

_____

4. Explain how this falls under the concept of "user-friendly."

_____

_____

_____

5. Explain the KeyListener interface.

_____

_____

_____

6. Identify the component that the KeyListener is being added to.

_____

_____

_____

7. Explain the purpose of requestFocus().

_____

_____

_____

8. Explain the getKeyText method.

_____

_____

_____

9. Explain the getKeyCode method.

_____

_____

_____

10. Explain the isActionKey method.

_____

_____

_____

11. Explain the getKeyChar method.

_____

_____

_____

12. Explain the following line of code:

```
label1.setText("Key Pressed: " + e.getKeyText(e.getKeyCode()));
```

_____

_____

_____

_____

_____

_____

_____

_____

13. Explain the following line of code:

```
        label2.setText("This key " + (e.isActionKey() ? " is " : " is not
") + "an action key.");
```

_____

_____

_____

_____

_____

_____

_____

_____

14. Explain the following line of code:

```
label1.setText("Key Typed: " + e.getKeyChar());
```

_____

_____

_____

_____

_____

_____

_____

Summary

You have now been exposed to many of the GUI components used within Java. However, keep in mind that there are many more that have not been covered. You must put some time and effort into experimenting and learning on your own with any programming language to which you are exposed.

In this lesson, you were introduced to three layout managers—FlowLayout, GridLayout, and BorderLayout. You were also shown how to remove the layout manager and to take control of the layout yourself using the setBounds method. This way you were able to place the components where you wanted them. The importance of the layout managers and the setBounds method was made apparent in Project 9-1 when your applet components overlaid each other. You also learned a great deal about GUI components. Finally, you learned the basics of mouse events and keyboard events. The need for mouse events is obvious. However, a lot of beginning programmers question the need for keyboard events. You should now be aware of the fact that using the keyboard is the only option for some computer users. Your programs should incorporate both types of events in order to address the needs of those who use the programs.

LESSON 9 REVIEW QUESTIONS

SHORT ANSWER

Define the following in the space provided.

1. Layout manager

_____

_____

_____

2. GUI

_____

_____

_____

3. FlowLayout

_____

_____

_____

4. Components

_____

_____

_____

5. Button

_____

_____

_____

6. Label

_____

_____

_____

7. GridLayout

_____

_____

_____

8. Check box

_____

_____

_____

9. Radio button

_____

_____

_____

10. BorderLayout

_____

_____

_____

11. NORTH, SOUTH, EAST, WEST, CENTER

_____

_____

_____

12. Mouse events

_____

_____

_____

13. Keyboard events

_____

_____

_____

14. Press

_____

_____

_____

15. Click

_____

_____

_____

16. Release

_____

_____

_____

17. Enter

_____

_____

_____

18. Exit

_____

_____

_____

19. Drag

_____

_____

_____

20. Move

_____

_____

_____

21. TextArea

_____

_____

_____

22. Word wrap

_____

_____

_____

23. CheckboxGroup

_____

_____

_____

24. Container

_____

_____

_____

25. setBounds()

_____

_____

_____

26. KeyListener

_____

_____

_____

27. ItemListener

_____

_____

_____

28. MouseListener

_____

_____

_____

29. MouseMotionListener

_____

_____

_____

30. Deprecate

_____

_____

_____

31. setVisible()

_____

_____

_____

32. Action key

_____

_____

_____

WRITTEN QUESTIONS

Write your answers to the following questions in the space provided.

1. Describe the differences between the layout managers.

_____

_____

_____

_____

2. Describe the difference between a TextField and a TextArea.

_____

_____

_____

_____

_____

_____

3. Explain the differences between the key event methods.

_____

_____

_____

_____

_____

_____

_____

4. Explain why only one component can be placed in each region of the BorderLayout.

_____

_____

_____

5. Explain how to convert a normal check box into a radio button.

_____

_____

_____

_____

_____

_____

6. Explain the differences between the mouse event methods.

_____

_____

_____

_____

_____

_____

_____

_____

_____

_____

_____

_____

_____

7. Explain why your applets should contain both mouse events and keyboard events.

_____

_____

_____

_____

_____

TESTING YOUR SKILLS

APPLICATION 9-1

Estimated Time:
Application 9-1 1 hour
Application 9-2 1 ¹/₂ hours
Application 9-3 3 hours

In Project 9-1, you coded an applet that used buttons and labels to demonstrate GUI components. The layout of your applet was not very organized because you used the default layout manager, FlowLayout.

It is your responsibility in this application to revisit your Project 9-1 applet and correct the layout. How you choose to correct the layout is up to you. You have multiple options available to you. The correct one will be the one that works.

1. Open **Proj9_1.java** and save it immediately as **App9_1.java**.

2. Modify the code so that the applet now appears organized on the screen.

3. Save your file.

4. Compile and run your applet. If you should encounter errors, correct them and then rerun your applet.

APPLICATION 9-2

In this application, you will rewrite Project 9-2 so that it uses radio buttons instead of normal check boxes.

1. Open **Proj9_2.java** and save it immediately as **App9_2.java**.

2. Modify the code so that the applet uses radio buttons instead of normal checkboxes.

3. Save your file.

4. Compile and run your applet. If you should encounter errors, correct them and then rerun your applet.

APPLICATION 9-3

Create an applet that uses mouse events and components. Choose the components that you would like to add to your applet, and then use mouse events to make something happen. Obviously, you have many components to choose from. Therefore, try to make your choices logically related to the purpose of your applet.

CRITICAL THINKING

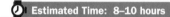
Estimated Time: 8–10 hours

Revisit each of the applets you have programmed in this book and choose three of them to which you will add both mouse events and keyboard events.

Remember that many people are not able to use a mouse and must use a keyboard. Your applets should incorporate both methods of interaction.

MULTIMEDIA

Introduction

One of the strengths of Java is its *multimedia* capabilities. Java is very capable in the area of manipulating *text*, *images*, *graphics*, and *audio*, as well as a combination of any of these components.

You will begin this lesson with loading and manipulating *images*. You will start with images provided to you, then you will experiment with creating your own using whatever programs you have at hand.

You will progress into *animating* the images by applying a *loop.* You will load one image then another, with a pause in between. This is the simplest of all animation methods—but it works!

You will also experiment with *audio*. As you have probably noticed, many Web pages are no longer solely text based; they now incorporate many, many types of media, including sound. You will learn how to load and play *audio clips*. You will also learn how to have the clip play once and how to have the clip loop throughout the execution of your applet.

Last, but not least, you will be exposed to *image maps*. Image maps are images that have *"hot areas"* that the user can click to cause something to happen. Usually when the mouse cursor is positioned over an image map a message appears in the status window informing the user of the action that will be performed.

So, let's get ready to have some fun!

This lesson will focus on the following:

- **Loading, manipulating, and displaying images.** You will begin by loading, manipulating, and displaying images provided for your use. Once you become familiar with the process, you will be encouraged to develop your own images with which to work.

- **Animating images.** You will simply loop your image. Looping is the process of loading one image, waiting, and then loading the next. Looping may result in jittery images, but it does the job.

- **Loading and playing audio clips.** You will be loading and playing audio clips and you will be adding the clips to existing applets. As you have probably noticed while browsing the Web, not many sites are purely text based anymore—most have multimedia characteristics.

- **Creating image maps.** Image maps allow the user to cause something to occur simply by clicking on the "hot areas" of an image. You should be familiar with image maps from the user's point of view. Now you will tackle them from the programmer's perspective.

PROJECT 10-1: Loading and Displaying Images Ⓑ

In this project you will create a simple applet that loads a simple image. The image is a rectangular object created in Microsoft Paint and saved in the **JPEG** (**Joint Photographic Experts Group**) format.

The applet will use the **getImage** method to load your image into the applet. This method takes two arguments. The **getDocumentBase** method is used to determine the location of the image and the image filename. Java assumes that the image is kept in the same location as the Web page that invoked the applet. The getImage method executes as a separate *thread*. This allows the applet to execute as the image is being loaded.

Once the image is loaded it is drawn on the applet using the Graphics method **drawImage**. You are responsible for informing drawImage as to what image is being drawn, at what coordinates it should be drawn, and onto which object. In this project the image will be drawn onto the applet.

The image files for each of the projects in this lesson are stored in the *Student Data & Resources* folder on the *Electronic Instructor* CD.

Step 1: Start Your Compiler

Start your compiler if it is not already running.

Step 2: Type in Your Code

Type in your code as follows. Save the file as **Proj10_1.java**.

```
// Proj10_1 Loading Images

import java.awt.*;
import java.applet.*;


public class Proj10_1 extends Applet
{
```

```
Image Hi;

public void init()
{
        Hi = getImage(getDocumentBase(), "Text.jpg");
}

public void paint(Graphics g)
{
        g.drawImage(Hi, 100, 100, this);
}

}
```

Step 3: Save Your Program

Once you have finished typing in your code, save it one final time before compiling your program.

Step 4: Compile and Run

Before running your applet, *copy* the **Text.jpg** file from the *Student Data & Resources* files to the same folder as your Proj10_1.java file. Otherwise, the applet will run but no image file will be displayed.

Enter the commands necessary to compile and run your program. If errors occur during the compile, check your code, correct any errors, and rerun the program.

Execute this applet maximized. Your applet should look similar to Figure 10-1.

FIGURE 10-1
Project 10-1 applet

Step 5: Review Your Code

Now that your program has run successfully answer the questions below.

1. Explain what happens when you first maximize the applet.

_____

_____

_____

2. Explain why the applet maximizes but the image is not displayed.

_____

_____

_____

3. Explain the getImage method.

_____

_____

_____

4. Explain the getDocumentBase method.

_____

_____

_____

5. Explain what happens when the applet is executed at various sizes.

_____

_____

_____

6. Explain the following line of code:

```
g.drawImage(Hi, 100, 100, this);
```

_____

_____

_____

_____

You have now loaded and displayed your first image. Now let's manipulate it.

PROJECT 10-2: Manipulating Images

As you discovered in the previous project, your images are loaded through separate threads of execution while the applet itself executes in its own thread. While this is convenient for keeping the user occupied, it does add to the processor's workload. Keep this in mind when adding images to your applets.

In this project you will load two separate JPEG files. Remember to make sure that these files are copied into the folder containing your Proj10_2.java file. Otherwise your images will not display. You will be working with two die faces created in Microsoft's Image Composer, which is included with Microsoft FrontPage. You will use another version of the drawImage method that allows you to manipulate the width and height of your image.

You will load and display the two images, and then display the images again at three times their original width and height.

Step 1: Start Your Compiler

Start your compiler if it is not already running.

Step 2: Type in Your Code

Type in your code as follows. Save the file as **Proj10_2.java**.

```java
// Proj10_2 Manipulating Images

import java.awt.*;
import java.applet.*;


public class Proj10_2 extends Applet
{
   Image Three, Five;

   public void init()
   {
        Three = getImage(getDocumentBase(), "Die3.jpg");
        Five = getImage(getDocumentBase(), "Die5.jpg");
   }

   public void paint(Graphics g)
   {
        g.drawImage(Three, 100, 100, this);
        g.drawImage(Five, 200, 100, this);

        int wide3 = Three.getWidth(this);
        int wide5 = Five.getWidth(this);
        int high3 = Three.getHeight(this);
        int high5 = Five.getHeight(this);
```

245

```
        g.drawImage(Three, 100, 200, wide3 * 3, high3 * 3, this);
        g.drawImage(Five, 300, 200, wide5 * 3, high5 * 3, this);

    }

}
```

Step 3: Save Your Program

Once you have finished typing in your code, save it one final time before compiling your program.

Step 4: Compile and Run

Before running your applet, *copy* the **Die3.jpg** file and the **Die5.jpg** from the *Student Data & Resources* files to the same folder as your Proj10_2.java file

Enter the commands necessary to compile and run your program. If errors occur during the compile, check your code, correct any errors, and rerun the program.

Make sure you test your program. Run this applet maximized. You will see the two images displayed at their normal width and height and then at three times their original width and height.

Your applet should look similar to Figure 10-2.

FIGURE 10-2
Project 10-2 applet

Step 5: Review Your Code

Now that your program has run successfully, review your code so that you understand the enhancements used in this project.

This applet is similar to the applet you created in Project 10-1. However, you used different images and then increased their size.

1. Explain what happens when the JPEG files are not saved in the same folder as the Java applet.

_____

_____

_____

2. Explain why the applet executes and then, after a short delay, the images are displayed.

_____

_____

_____

_____

_____

3. Explain what a separate thread of execution means.

_____

_____

_____

4. Explain the following line of code:

```
Three = getImage(getDocumentBase(), "Die3.jpg");
```

_____

_____

5. Explain why it takes the images longer to load in this applet than your Proj10_1.java applet.

_____

_____

_____

6. Explain the following lines of code:

```
int wide3 = Three.getWidth(this);
int high3 = Three.getHeight(this);
```

_____

7. Explain the following line of code:

```
g.drawImage(Three, 100, 200, wide3 * 3, high3 * 3, this);
```

Your applet should execute similarly to the one you created in Project 10-1. Keep in mind the difference in delay in loading each applet. The more images included in your applet and the more complex the images, the longer the applet will take to execute.

PROJECT 10-3: Image Loop   Ⓑ

In this project you will use the same die faces that you used in Project 10-2 to create an image loop. This time you will use all six die faces.

You will begin by creating an image array. During the init method you will "get" your images from the folder in which they are stored. As before they should all be in this project folder. You will use a for loop to "get" your images. During the start method you will make sure that you are beginning with the first image, die number one (remember that computers start counting with 0).

The paint method will be used to display the die faces. In fact, you will use four different draw-Image methods to draw four separate image loops. You will "step," or loop, through the images in order to simulate motion. You will cause the applets execution thread to **"sleep,"** or pause, for a number of milliseconds in order to pace the animation. Image looping comes with an inherent problem. The more complex the image, the more noticeable the jumps between images.

Finally, you will add a small section of **exception handling** code. The **try** block designates the sleep method as the line of code that may **throw** an **exception**. This simply means that it may cause an error. If it does, then the **catch** block executes, but only if it is an interruption exception. What does it do for us? It simply displays a text string informing us as to what the error is.

Let's get animated!

Step 1: Start Your Compiler

Start your compiler if it is not already running.

Step 2: Type in Your Code

Type in your code as follows. Save the file as **Proj10_3.java**.

```
// Proj10_3 Image Loop

import java.awt.*;
import java.applet.*;


public class Proj10_3 extends Applet
{
   Image Dice[];
   int totalDice = 6, currentDice = 0, sleepDice = 1000;

   public void init()
   {
        Dice = new Image[totalDice];

        for (int ctr = 0; ctr < Dice.length; ctr++)
                Dice[ctr] = getImage(getDocumentBase(), "Die" + (ctr + 1) +
".jpg");
   }

   public void start()
   {
        currentDice = 0;
   }

   public void paint(Graphics g)
   {
        g.drawImage(Dice[currentDice], 100, 100, this);

        g.drawImage(Dice[currentDice], 100, 200, this);

        g.drawImage(Dice[currentDice], 200, 100, this);

        g.drawImage(Dice[currentDice], 200, 200, this);

        currentDice = (currentDice + 1) % totalDice;

        try
        {
                Thread.sleep(sleepDice);
        }

        catch(InterruptedException e)
        {
```

```
                showStatus(e.toString());
        }

        repaint();
    }

}
```

Step 3: Save Your Program

Once you have finished typing in your code, save it one final time before compiling your program.

Step 4: Compile and Run

Before running your applet, *copy* the **Die1.jpg**, **Die2.jpg**, **Die3.jpg**, **Die4.jpg**, **Die5.jpg**, and **Die6.jpg** files from the *Student Data & Resources* files to the same folder as your Proj10_3.java file.

Enter the commands necessary to compile and run your program. If errors occur during the compile, check your code, correct any errors, and rerun the program.

Make sure you test your program. Run this applet maximized. You will see four groups of dice rotating through their sequence. The sleep time period is set to 1,000 milliseconds, which is equal to one second. Each group of dice should slowly "rotate" through the sequence.

As you experiment with your applet, decrease the sleep time value from 1,000 to a much smaller amount in order to make the flicker problem that comes with image looping more apparent.

Your applet should look similar to Figure 10-3.

FIGURE 10-3
Project 10-3 applet

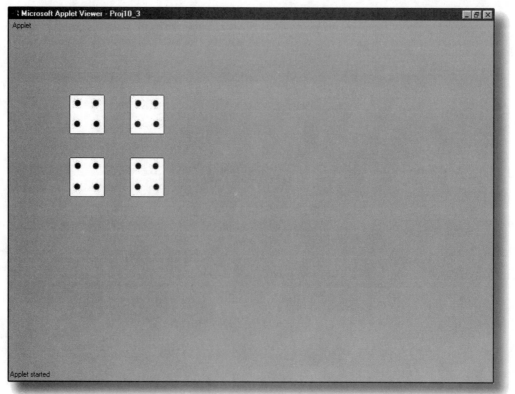

Step 5: Review Your Code

Now that your program has run successfully, review your code so that you understand the enhancements used in this project.

1. Explain what happens when the applet starts.

_____

_____

_____

2. Explain what happens when the applet initializes.

_____

_____

_____

_____

3. Explain why an array is used to hold the images as they are loaded.

_____

_____

_____

4. Explain the following variable declarations and initializations.

```
int totalDice = 6, currentDice = 0, sleepDice = 1000;
```

_____

_____

_____

_____

_____

5. Explain the init method. The code is shown below.

```
public void init()
{
      Dice = new Image[totalDice];

      for (int ctr = 0; ctr < Dice.length; ctr++)
           Dice[ctr] = getImage(getDocumentBase(), "Die" + (ctr + 1) +
".jpg");
}
```

_____

_____

_____

_____

_____

_____

_____

6. Explain the following line of code:

```
g.drawImage(Dice[currentDice], 100, 100, this);
```

_____

_____

_____

7. Explain the following line of code.

```
currentDice = (currentDice + 1) % totalDice;
```

_____

_____

_____

8. Explain the try and catch blocks of code. The code is shown below.

```
try
{
        Thread.sleep(sleepDice);
}

catch(InterruptedException e)
{
        showStatus(e.toString());
}
```

_____

_____

_____

_____

_____

9. Explain what happens when `repaint()` is called.

_____

_____

_____

_____

_____

_____

10. Calling `repaint()` in this manner causes a problem with screen flicker. Explain what causes the problem of flicker to occur.

_____

_____

_____

_____

_____

_____

_____

_____

You have now created a simple image loop. Take some time to experiment with images of your own creation.

P R O J E C T   1 0 - 4 :
Loading and Playing Audio Clips

Ⓑ

This project introduces the technique of loading and playing *audio clips*. You will be using a similar get method to the one used to "get" your images. The ***getAudioClip*** method will be used to load your audio (*.au*) files. These files are available on the Electronic Instructor CD.

You will be loading and playing two different audio clips. They must be saved in your project folder just like the image files were in the earlier projects. You will be adding buttons that call the ***play, loop***, and ***stop*** methods that belong to the ***AudioClip*** object.

Let's make some noise!

Step 1: Start Your Compiler

Start your compiler if it is not already running.

Step 2: Type in Your Code

Type in your code as follows. Save the file as **Proj10_4.java**.

```
// Proj10_4 Audio Clips

import java.awt.*;
import java.applet.*;
import java.awt.event.*;


public class Proj10_4 extends Applet implements ActionListener
{
    AudioClip noise1, noise2;
    Button playNoise1, loopNoise1, stopNoise1, playNoise2, loopNoise2,
stopNoise2;

    public void init()
    {
        setLayout(null);

        noise1 = getAudioClip(getDocumentBase(),
"tiptoe.thru.the.tulips.au");
        noise2 = getAudioClip(getDocumentBase(), "ip.au");

        playNoise1 = new Button("Play Tiptoe");
        playNoise1.setBounds(30, 30, 80, 20);
        add(playNoise1);
        playNoise1.addActionListener(this);

        loopNoise1 = new Button("Loop Tiptoe");
        loopNoise1.setBounds(130, 30, 80, 20);
        add(loopNoise1);
        loopNoise1.addActionListener(this);

        stopNoise1 = new Button("Stop Tiptoe");
        stopNoise1.setBounds(230, 30, 80, 20);
        add(stopNoise1);
        stopNoise1.addActionListener(this);

        playNoise2 = new Button("Play Ip");
        playNoise2.setBounds(30, 60, 80, 20);
        add(playNoise2);
        playNoise2.addActionListener(this);

        loopNoise2 = new Button("Loop Ip");
        loopNoise2.setBounds(130, 60, 80, 20);
```

```
        add(loopNoise2);
        loopNoise2.addActionListener(this);

        stopNoise2 = new Button("Stop Ip");
        stopNoise2.setBounds(230, 60, 80, 20);
        add(stopNoise2);
        stopNoise2.addActionListener(this);

    }

    public void actionPerformed(ActionEvent e)
    {
        if (e.getSource() == playNoise1)
            noise1.play();

        if(e.getSource() == loopNoise1)
            noise1.loop();

        if (e.getSource() == stopNoise1)
            noise1.stop();

        if (e.getSource() == playNoise2)
            noise2.play();

        if(e.getSource() == loopNoise2)
            noise2.loop();

        if (e.getSource() == stopNoise2)
            noise2.stop();

    }
}
```

Step 3: Save Your Program

Once you have finished typing in your code, save it one final time before compiling your program.

Step 4: Compile and Run

Before running your applet, copy the **tiptoe.thru.the.tulips.au** file and the **ip.au** files from the *Student Data & Resources* files to the same folder as your Proj10_4.java file.

Enter the commands necessary to compile and run your program. If errors occur during the compile, check your code, correct any errors, and rerun the program.

Make sure you test your program. Run this applet maximized. You will see the two sets of buttons displayed toward the top of the applet. Each set of buttons corresponds to one of the two audio clips that were loaded.

You will hear each sound play once if you click either of the Play buttons. The sounds will loop if you click either of the Loop buttons, and of course, the sound will stop once you click either of the Stop buttons.

Your applet should look similar to Figure 10-4.

FIGURE 10-4

Project 10-4 applet

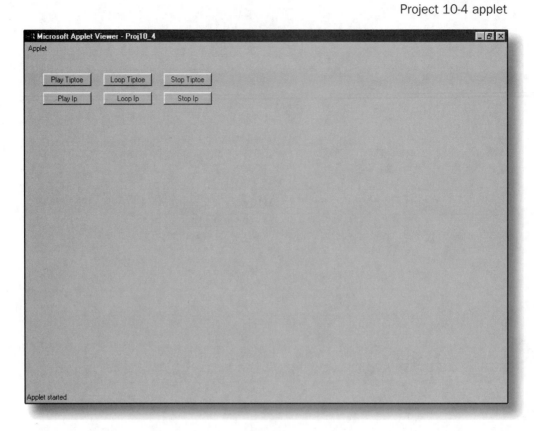

Step 5: Review Your Code

Now that your program has run successfully, review your code so that you understand the enhancements used in this project.

1. Explain when the audio clips load.

_____

_____

_____

2. Explain why audio clips are used. Can *.wav* or *.mid* files be used in place of the audio clips?

_____

_____

_____

3. Explain the following line of code.

```
        noise1 = getAudioClip(getDocumentBase(),
"tiptoe.thru.the.tulips.au");
```

_____

_____

256

4. Explain the following lines of code:

```
if (e.getSource() == playNoise1)
    noise1.play();
```

5. Explain the following lines of code:

```
if(e.getSource() == loopNoise1)
    noise1.loop();
```

6. Explain the following lines of code:

```
if (e.getSource() == stopNoise1)
    noise1.stop();
```

You have now learned how to add audio clips to your applets.

PROJECT 10-5 : Image Maps   B

This project deals with creating ***image maps***. Image maps help create more interesting Web pages by allowing the user to gain information from the page simply by placing the mouse over one of the components. Obviously mouse events will come into play with image maps—if only by placing your mouse cursor over an image.

In this project you will display messages based on which part of the image to which the user points the mouse. Of course, you can become very slick in adding multiple events to these types of images, but that's down the road. Let's start simple and make sure we get it right!

Step 1: Start Your Compiler

Start your compiler if it is not already running.

Step 2: Type in Your Code

Type in your code as follows. Save the file as **Proj10_5.java**.

```
// Proj10_5 Image Map

import java.awt.*;
import java.awt.event.*;
import java.applet.Applet;


public class Proj10_5 extends Applet implements MouseListener,
MouseMotionListener
{
   Image mapImage;
   MediaTracker trackImage;
   int width, height;

   public void init()
   {
        addMouseListener(this);
        addMouseMotionListener(this);
        trackImage = new MediaTracker(this);
        mapImage = getImage(getDocumentBase(), "DiceImage.jpg");
        trackImage.addImage(mapImage, 0);

        try
        {
            trackImage.waitForAll();
        }

        catch(InterruptedException e)
        {
            // Empty
        }

        width = mapImage.getWidth(this);
        height = mapImage.getHeight(this);
        resize(width, height);
   }

   public void paint(Graphics g)
   {
        g.drawImage(mapImage, 0, 0, this);
   }

   public void mouseClicked(MouseEvent e)
   {
   }
```

```
public void mousePressed(MouseEvent e)
{
}

public void mouseReleased(MouseEvent e)
{
}

public void mouseEntered(MouseEvent e)
{
}

public void mouseExited(MouseEvent e)
{
    showStatus("Pointer outside of DiceImage.");
}

public void mouseDragged(MouseEvent e)
{
}

public void mouseMoved(MouseEvent e)
{
    showStatus(translateLocation(e.getX()));
}

public String translateLocation(int x)
{
    int imagewidth = width / 6;

    if (x >= 0 && x <= imagewidth)
        return "One";

    else if (x > imagewidth && x < imagewidth * 2)
        return "Two";

    else if (x > imagewidth * 2 && x < imagewidth * 3)
        return "Three";

    else if (x > imagewidth * 3 && x < imagewidth * 4)
        return "Four";

    else if (x > imagewidth * 4 && x < imagewidth * 5)
        return "Five";

    else if (x > imagewidth * 5 && x < imagewidth * 6)
        return "Six";

    return "";
}
}
```

Step 3: Save Your Program

Once you have finished typing in your code, save it one final time before compiling your program.

Step 4: Compile and Run

Before running your applet, *copy* the **Dice Image.jpg** file from the *Student Data & Resources* files to the same folder as your Proj10_5.java file

Enter the commands necessary to compile and run your program. If errors occur during the compile, check your code, correct any errors, and rerun the program.

Make sure you test your program. This applet will size itself. You will see the mouse events and the coordinates at which the events occur displayed in the status window of your applet. Experiment with the two mouse events. Basically the user receives information as he or she moves the mouse across the image map.

Run your applet at a size similar to Figure 10-5. The various events will display on the face of your applet.

FIGURE 10-5
Project 10-5 applet

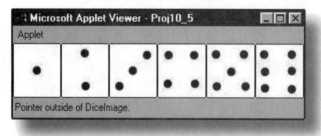

Step 5: Review Your Code

Now that your program has run successfully, review your code so that you understand the enhancements used in this project.

1. Explain why the applet sizes itself.

_____

_____

_____

2. Explain the variable declarations shown below.

```
Image mapImage;
MediaTracker trackImage;
int width, height;
```

_____

_____

_____

_____

_____

3. Explain the difference between MouseListener and MouseMotionListener interfaces.

_____

_____

_____

4. Explain why each of the methods must be defined when implementing both of the above interfaces.

_____

_____

_____

5. Explain the following lines of code and their relationship to each other:

```
trackImage = new MediaTracker(this);
mapImage = getImage(getDocumentBase(), "DiceImage.jpg");
trackImage.addImage(mapImage, 0);
```

_____

_____

_____

_____

_____

_____

_____

_____

_____

6. Explain what component the mouse listeners are added to.

_____

_____

_____

7. Explain the following block of code:

```
try
{
    trackImage.waitForAll();
}

catch(InterruptedException e)
{
    // Empty
}
```

_____

_____

_____

_____

_____

_____

8. Explain the following block of code:

```
width = mapImage.getWidth(this);
height = mapImage.getHeight(this);
resize(width, height);
```

_____

_____

_____

_____

_____

_____

9. Explain the paint method.

```
public void paint(Graphics g)
{
        g.drawImage(mapImage, 0, 0, this);
}
```

_____

_____

_____

_____

10. Explain the following mouse events:

```
public void mouseExited(MouseEvent e)
{
        showStatus("Pointer outside of DiceImage.");
}

public void mouseMoved(MouseEvent e)
{
        showStatus(translateLocation(e.getX()));
}
```

_____

_____

_____

_____

_____

_____

_____

_____

11. Explain the following method:

```java
public String translateLocation(int x)
{
        int imagewidth = width / 6;

        if (x >= 0 && x <= imagewidth)
            return "One";

        else if (x > imagewidth && x < imagewidth * 2)
          return "Two";

        else if (x > imagewidth * 2 && x < imagewidth * 3)
            return "Three";

        else if (x > imagewidth * 3 && x < imagewidth * 4)
            return "Four";

        else if (x > imagewidth * 4 && x < imagewidth * 5)
            return "Five";

        else if (x > imagewidth * 5 && x < imagewidth * 6)
            return "Six";

        return "";
}
```

_____

_____

_____

_____

_____

_____

_____

_____

Summary

This lesson exposed you to Java's multimedia capabilities. The ones you have been introduced to in this lesson will enhance your applets immediately. However, don't quit now—Java has many more multimedia capabilities.

In this lesson, you were introduced to loading and displaying images. From loading and displaying you moved into manipulating. You took a simple image and expanded its size.

You also learned how to loop images. Looping images is the easiest way to create animations. You then learned how to add audio clips to your applet. Make sure you revisit some of your earlier applets and add sound to them.

Finally, you learned the basics of image maps and how they interact with mouse events. Now it should be obvious to you the importance of creating applets with multimedia capabilities and characteristics—it's what people expect!

LESSON 10 REVIEW QUESTIONS

SHORT ANSWER

Define the following in the space provided.

1. Multimedia

2. Text

3. Images

4. Graphics

5. Audio

_____

_____

_____

6. Animation

_____

_____

_____

7. Loop

_____

_____

_____

8. Audio clip

_____

_____

_____

9. Image map

_____

_____

_____

10. Hot areas

_____

_____

_____

11. JPEG

_____

_____

_____

12. Mouse events

_____

_____

_____

13. Thread

_____

_____

_____

14. Sleep

_____

_____

_____

15. Try

_____

_____

_____

16. Throw

_____

_____

_____

17. Catch

_____

_____

_____

18. Exception handling

_____

_____

_____

19. Play

_____

_____

_____

20. Stop

_____

_____

_____

21. MouseListener

_____

_____

_____

22. MouseMotionListener

_____

_____

_____

WRITTEN QUESTIONS

Write your answers to the following questions in the space provided.

1. Describe the difference between adding images and adding audio to your applet.

_____

_____

_____

_____

_____

_____

_____

_____

2. Explain how looping works.

_____

_____

_____

_____

_____

_____

_____

_____

3. Explain why only .au files can be used with an AudioClip object.

_____

_____

_____

4. Explain the difference between the AudioClip play and loop methods.

5. Explain how image maps work.

6. Explain the difference between the mouse event methods.

7. Explain hot areas.

_____

_____

_____

_____

_____

8. Explain the relationship between image maps and mouse events.

_____

_____

_____

_____

_____

CRITICAL THINKING

ACTIVITY 10-1

Estimated Time:
Activity 10-1 8–10 hours
Activity 10-2 8–10 hours

SCANS This Critical Thinking exercise should be fun. Instead of us telling you what to design, you decide. Design an applet that includes each of the techniques used in this lesson. You are responsible for designing and creating both the image and the audio files to go with the applets.

ACTIVITY 10-2

SCANS Choose three of the applets you have programmed in this course and add multimedia capabilities to them. Remember that your applets should be user-friendly, so don't add the multimedia components to just any applet. Add them where they will enhance your work.

INDEX

273